DAILY TIMES TABLES TEASERS FOR AGES 5–7

WHAT IS *DAILY TIMES TABLES TEASERS*?

Daily Times Tables Teasers 5–7 is a collection of activities designed to develop children's knowledge, skills and understanding in multiplication. The activities are directly linked to the requirements of the Primary Framework for mathematics for Key Stage 1.

The times tables teasers include games, rhymes, practical investigations and simple problem-solving tasks. The ideas are designed to be used flexibly and many can be easily adapted to reflect children's particular interests or to make cross curricular links. In addition, most of the activities can be easily differentiated to cater for differing ability levels within a class.

HOW IS IT ORGANISED?

It is widely accepted that teachers need to use a range of presentation styles and teaching materials to ensure that all children are given the opportunity to learn through their preferred learning style.

The times table teasers are organised into four chapters, each focusing on a different learning style:
1. Visual (seeing)
2. Auditory (hearing)
3. Tactile (touching)
4. Kinaesthetic (moving)

WHAT DOES EACH TIME TABLE TEASER CONTAIN?

To make the book easy to use, all the times table teasers follow the same format.

Learning objectives: Each times tables teaser addresses one or more of the NNS objectives from either Year 1 or Year 2.

Learning link: Many of the activities are multi-sensory. Links to other learning styles are listed in this section.

Organisation: Each times tables teaser gives suggestions for organisation, for example whole class/small group. However, many of the ideas can be easily adapted for individual circumstances.

Resources: The resources needed to implement an activity are listed in this section.

What to do: Clear, step by step instructions are given for carrying out the activity. Emphasis is placed on active participation by the children through, for example, the use of games and practical apparatus. Where appropriate, suggested questions and opportunities for teacher interventions are also included.

Now try this: At the end of each times tables teaser, suggestions have been given for how to further develop or adapt the ideas in future lessons.

HOW TO USE THE ACTIVITIES

The times tables teasers are designed to provide ideas for short, purposeful activities that cater for the range of learning styles. They can be used in a number of ways.

1. Develop a daily times table teaser time, for example at the start of each day or after lunch.

2. Incorporate times table teasers into the daily maths lesson.

3. Choose an activity from each chapter in rotation or plan to focus on a different learning style each week to ensure that all learning styles are given equal coverage.

4. Many of the activities are teacher-led; others can be given to the children themselves for self-directed learning. It may also be appropriate for teaching assistants working within a class to conduct activities with smaller groups of children.

MULTIPLICATION MACHINE 1

OBJECTIVE: to begin to derive and recall multiplication facts for the two-times tables

LEARNING LINK: auditory

ORGANISATION: whole class or adult-led groups

RESOURCES: two sets of small number cards (0–10, even numbers 0–20); a simple multiplication machine (see below)

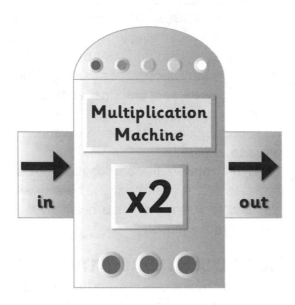

WHAT TO DO

● The 0–10 cards are on the board; the 0–20 cards are in the multiplication machine.

● Find out how the multiplication machine works: select a number card from the board, for example, 2. Put the card into the machine. Let the machine whirr away for a few seconds. What number will come out the other side?

● Look at the writing on the front of the machine. What operation has the multiplication machine performed on the number? (It multiplies by 2.)

● What happens to other numbers between 0 and 10 when you put them into the machine? (Allow different children to operate the machine.)

NOW TRY THIS

1. Make your own simple multiplication machines from junk materials.

2. Make a multiplication machine that multiplies numbers by 5 or 10.

MULTIPLICATION MACHINE 2

OBJECTIVE: to begin to derive and recall multiplication facts for the two-, five-, ten-times tables

LEARNING LINK: auditory

ORGANISATION: whole class, working in pairs

RESOURCES: sets of number cards: 0–10, multiples of 2–20, multiples of 5–50, multiples of 10–100; a simple multiplication machine (see left) with '× 10' on the front of the box (the writing should be concealed with a sticky note)

WHAT TO DO

● The multiplication machine is a special machine that can change numbers. The machine can be set to multiply any number that is put into it by 2, 5 or 10.

● Work in pairs to work out which setting the machine is switched to today.

● If you put the number 5 into the machine, which number comes out the other side? If you put number 6 into the machine, which number comes out the other side?

● Discuss your observations with a partner. Decide whether the multiplication machine has been set to multiply by 2, 5 or 10.

● When the sticky note is removed to reveal the answer, check if you are right.

● The multiplication machine has changed setting. Which setting is it on now?

NOW TRY THIS

Play a 'Show me' game. When a number is put into the machine, hold up a card to show what number you think will come out the other side.

SORT IT OUT

OBJECTIVE: to begin to derive two-digit multiples of 2, 5 and 10

LEARNING LINK: tactile

ORGANISATION: groups of three or four

RESOURCES: a giant sorting sheet (see below); a set of number cards showing two-digit multiples of 2 and 5 for each group

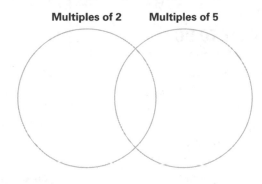

Multiples of 2   Multiples of 5

WHAT TO DO

● Each group has a sorting sheet and a set of number cards. Read the labels on the sheet. Discuss what they mean.

● Sort the number cards into the appropriate section of the Venn diagram according to whether they are a multiple of 2, 5, or both 2 and 5.

● Look carefully at the numbers in each section of the diagram. Can you see any patterns? For example: all even multiples of 5 are also multiples of 2; numbers that are multiples of 10 are also multiples of 2 and 5.

NOW TRY THIS

'Quick sort': race against the other groups. Who can sort their number cards first?

MULTIPLE FOOTBALL

OBJECTIVE: to recognise multiples of 2, 5 and 10

LEARNING LINK: tactile

ORGANISATION: groups of three or four

RESOURCES: photocopiable page 56: Multiple football gameboard; a set of football counters numbered 1–30 for each group.

WHAT TO DO

● Talk about multiples of 2, 5 and 10. Remember that a number may be a multiple of more than one number. For example, 20 is a multiple of 2, 5 and 10.

● Each group has a gameboard and a set of football counters. Shuffle the counters and spread them face down on the table.

● Take it in turns to pick up a football, look at the number and place it in the correct goal. If the number does not belong in any goal, that is, it is not a multiple of 2, 5 or 10, you must keep it.

● The winner is the player with the fewest footballs at the end of the game.

NOW TRY THIS

1. 'Quick sort': sort the footballs into the correct goals as quickly as you can.

2. Try playing with football counters numbered with three-digit numbers. Identify which of the numbers are multiples of 2, 5 or 10.

TREASURE ISLAND

OBJECTIVE: to derive and recall multiplication facts for the two- and ten-times tables

LEARNING LINK: tactile

ORGANISATION: pairs

RESOURCES: photocopiable page 57: Treasure island; coloured crayons

WHAT TO DO

● Each pair has a treasure map, a set of clues and a coloured crayon. The clues will lead you to a location on the island where there is buried treasure.

● Work out the answer to the first clue, locate the square on the grid with that number in it and then mark the square with a coloured cross.

● Work out the answer to the remaining clues and record the pathway to the treasure by drawing a line from one answer to the next until the last clue has been solved.

● There may be a prize for those who have followed the correct path to the treasure.

NOW TRY THIS

Draw your own treasure map. Write a set of clues to lead your partner to the treasure.

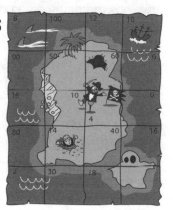

TRAIN RIDE

OBJECTIVE: to improve ability to count in tens; to begin to understand that multiplication is repeated addition

LEARNING LINK: tactile

ORGANISATION: whole class

RESOURCES: a laminated picture of a train or a small model train; a train track on the board marked with ten stations (each station should have an imaginative name)

WHAT TO DO

● Count the stations on the train track. Read out what each station is called. There is a distance of 10 miles between each station.

● Move the train from the start to the first station. Write down how many miles the train has travelled. Move the train to the next station. Work out how far the train has travelled now. Write 10 + 10 on the board. Continue until the train has reached the end of the track and the number sentence reads 10 + 10 + 10 + 10 + 10 + 10 + 10 + 10 + 10 + 10.

● Work in pairs to solve some problems. For example: The train has travelled 40 miles – which station has it reached? How do you know?

NOW TRY THIS

Complete the activities above using a picture of a motorway with 10 service stations and a distance of 5 miles between each.

GROWING WILD

OBJECTIVE: to understand that multiplication is repeated addition

LEARNING LINK: tactile

ORGANISATION: whole class, working in pairs

RESOURCES: photocopiable page 58: Growing wild; a picture of a plant; 30cm rulers; paper and pencils; a green whiteboard pen

WHAT TO DO

● Look at the picture of a plant on the board.

● In pairs, use paper, pencils and rulers to try to solve the following problem:

On Monday, the plant was 5cm tall. Every day it grew 5cm taller. How tall was the plant on Saturday? Record your answer on the photocopiable sheet.

● Share your answer with the class. Come out to the board. Draw a scale picture of the plant on each day.

● Record the calculation as a number sentence: 5 + 5 + 5 + 5 + 5 + 5 = 30cm. Say together, *6 lots of 5 makes 30.*

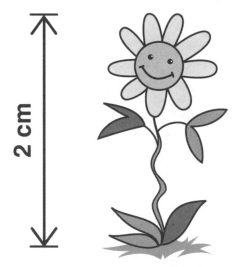

NOW TRY THIS

Try other simple problems where you need to count in twos, fives or tens. For example, investigate problems involving increases in capacity, time or weight.

JUMPING

OBJECTIVE: to understand that multiplication is repeated addition
LEARNING LINK: tactile
ORGANISATION: whole class, working in pairs
RESOURCES: a video recording of a show-jumping or cross-country competition; paper and pencils

WHAT TO DO
● Watch a short section of the video. Make a tally to record how many fences the horse jumps over.
● Award the horse 2 points for each fence jumped.
● Record the calculation as a number sentence, for example: 2 + 2 + 2 + 2 + 2 = 10 points. Say together, *5 lots of 2 makes 10*.
● Repeat for a different number of jumps. Try to record your own number sentences.

NOW TRY THIS
1 Award 5 or 10 points for each jump.
2. Watch clips of other sports to generate a tally, for example a hurdles race or a rally in a tennis match.

WRAPPING PAPER ARRAYS

OBJECTIVE: to understand multiplication as representing an array
LEARNING LINK: tactile
ORGANISATION: pairs
RESOURCES: several sheets of wrapping paper with designs, for example rows of spots/balloons (cut out sections of wrapping paper to show simple rectangular arrays, for example 4 × 2, 3 × 2)

WHAT TO DO
● Each pair has several pieces of wrapping paper. Look at your first piece. Describe the array. For example, *There are six rows of balloons with two balloons in each row*. Count in twos to calculate how many balloons there are altogether.
● Write a number sentence to describe the array (6 × 2 = 12).
● Look at the other pieces of wrapping paper. Write a number sentence to describe each array.

NOW TRY THIS
Look at the number sentence written on the board. Work out which wrapping paper array it describes.

TARGET NUMBER

OBJECTIVE: to use the signs × and = to describe and solve a problem
LEARNING LINK: tactile
ORGANISATION: individuals, pairs
RESOURCES: paper and pencils, counters, cubes or other small counting apparatus; number lines

WHAT TO DO
● Look at the target number on the board, for example 20. Think of a multiplication calculation that equals 20. Work as a class to record suggestions on the board as number sentences, for example 2 × 10 or 4 × 5.
● Repeat the activity with different numbers.
● Working on your own or in pairs, write down a number sentence for each target number on the board.
● You can use practical apparatus or number lines to help.

NOW TRY THIS
Play a game of 'Show me'. Your teacher writes a target number on the board. The first person to hold up a multiplication sentence that equals the target number is the winner.

CRACK THE CODE

OBJECTIVE: to derive and recall multiplication facts for the two-, five- and ten-times tables
LEARNING LINK: auditory
ORGANISATION: pairs
RESOURCES: photocopiable page 59: Crack the code; a whiteboard and pen for each pair; stickers, sweets or other small rewards

WHAT TO DO

● Look at the following number sentences on the board:
3×10, 9×5, 7×5, 6×2, 4×4, 9×2.
● The questions are clues. If you solve them you will crack a secret code and possibly win a prize.
● Solve the clues. Find each answer on the photocopiable page. Draw the corresponding shapes on your whiteboard in the correct order.
● Ask your teacher to check your answer. You may win a prize if you crack the code correctly.

NOW TRY THIS

1. Try cracking a longer code.
2. Devise your own code for your partner to solve.

MISSING NUMBERS

OBJECTIVE: to count on in steps of two
LEARNING LINK: auditory
ORGANISATION: whole class, working in pairs
RESOURCES: paper and pencils

WHAT TO DO

● Look at the series of numbers on the board. For example, 12, 14, 18, 22, 24, 26, 30.
● The numbers are supposed to go up in steps of 2, but some numbers have been missed out.
● In pairs, write down the number sequence. Work together and try to fill in the missing numbers.

● Help your teacher to correct the number sequence on the board. Discuss as a class whether all the missing numbers have been identified correctly. Finally, check the answer on the class number line.
● Repeat the activity using a different set of numbers.

NOW TRY THIS

Repeat the activity with a series of numbers that increases in steps of 5 or 10.

TENS RACE

OBJECTIVE: to learn how to count in tens more quickly; to recognise two-digit multiples of ten
LEARNING LINK: kinaesthetic
ORGANISATION: whole class; pairs
RESOURCES: a set of number cards showing multiples of 10 up to 100 for every child; a counting stick

WHAT TO DO

● As a class, count in tens in your heads as your teacher points to each division on the counting stick. Pause at different points, to check what number has been reached, or to predict what the next number will be.
● Your teacher spreads a set of number cards face-up on the floor. As a class, order the multiples of 10 in ascending order. Notice the pattern of 1, 2, 3, 4 within the numbers.
● In pairs, play the 'Tens race'. Each of you has a shuffled set of number cards. The aim is to try to be the first person to arrange their number cards in ascending order.
● Play the game several times. Choose a new opponent each time.

NOW TRY THIS

1. Use the number cards to play a 'Show me' game. For example: Show me the number that is 7 lots of 10. Show me the missing number: 20 30 __ 50.
2. Play 'Fives race' and 'Twos race', using multiples of 5 and 2.

WHAT'S WRONG?

OBJECTIVE: to derive and recall multiplication facts for the ten-times table
LEARNING LINK: auditory
ORGANISATION: whole class, working in pairs
RESOURCES: paper and pencils

WHAT TO DO

● Look at the list of multiplications on the board, some of which are incorrect. For example:

$2 \times 10 = 20$
$7 \times 10 = 70$
$8 \times 10 = 90$
$3 \times 10 = 30$
$10 \times 10 = 20$

● In pairs, work out which calculations are incorrect.
● Come out to the board to draw a smiley face next to the multiplications that you think are correct and a sad face next to those that you think are incorrect.
● Write corrections to the multiplications you identified to be wrong.

NOW TRY THIS

1. Repeat the activity using facts (some incorrect) for the two- or five-times tables.
2. For a challenge, correct a mixed list of calculations (some incorrect) for the two-, five- and ten-times tables.

COUNTING STICK

OBJECTIVE: to improve ability to count in fives; to use the symbols × and = to describe and solve a problem
LEARNING LINK: auditory
ORGANISATION: whole class
RESOURCES: a counting stick; a small finger puppet or toy; Velcro (for Now Try This)

WHAT TO DO

● Count in fives as the finger puppet jumps on each division on the counting stick.

● Repeat. This time, count in your head. The finger puppet pauses at several points. Your teacher asks various children to say which number the toy is resting on.
● Watch the puppet carefully as it jumps to the fourth division on the counting stick. How many jumps has it made? What number has it landed on? One of you will record the calculation as a number sentence on the board:

$4 \times 5 = 20.$

● Repeat the activity several times. Different children record the calculations on the board.

NOW TRY THIS

Your teacher sticks number cards, showing the multiples of 5 to 50, onto the counting stick. Order the cards correctly. One will be removed. Work out the missing number.

QUICK SHUFFLE

OBJECTIVE: to use the symbols × and = to describe and solve a problem
LEARNING LINK: kinaesthetic
ORGANISATION: whole class, working in pairs
RESOURCES: small whiteboards and pens; sets of large number and symbol cards, for example 5, 2, 10, ×, = or 7, 5, 35, ×, =

WHAT TO DO

● Five children stand at the front. Each child holds up a card, for example 5, 2, 10, ×, =.
● In pairs, look carefully at the numbers and symbols being held up. Consider what number sentence can be made by shuffling the order of the cards. Write the number sentence on your whiteboard.
● One pair comes to the front. They shuffle the children holding cards into the right order. They describe what they have done and why.
● As a class, discuss whether the order is correct. Are there any alternative answers?

NOW TRY THIS

Try working in groups with a similar set of cards. Play 'Quick shuffle': order your cards correctly as quickly as possible.

TIMES TABLES PAIRS

OBJECTIVE: to begin to derive and recall multiplication facts for the five-times table

LEARNING LINK: kinaesthetic

ORGANISATION: groups of four or five

RESOURCES: two sets of cards for each group (set 1: calculations for the five-times tables from 0 × 5 to 10 × 5; set 2: multiples of 5 from 0–50) (each set of cards should be a different colour)

WHAT TO DO

● Play 'Times tables pairs': spread out two sets of cards face down on the floor. Turn over two cards, one of each colour. Can the cards be put together to make a complete calculation (a pair)? If they can, the player keeps them; if not, the cards are returned face down to the floor.

● You are the winner if you collect more cards than your friends by the end of the game.

NOW TRY THIS

1. Shuffle several sets of cards together. Use them to play 'Times tables snap'.

2. Have a race. Which group can be first to match each calculation with the correct answer?

ROLL IT ON

OBJECTIVE: to practise recall of multiplication facts for the two-times table, up to 6 × 2

LEARNING LINK: tactile

ORGANISATION: whole class

RESOURCES: a large foam dice (1–6 spots)

WHAT TO DO

● The whole class sits in a circle. The dice is rolled to one of the children, who multiplies the number of spots on it by 2. They recall the multiplication fact as quickly as they can and then roll the dice to someone else in the circle.

● Continue until everyone in the circle has had at least one turn.

● You can calculate the answer by counting on in twos for the number you have rolled.

NOW TRY THIS

1. Practise quick recall of multiplication facts up to 12 × 2. Play 'Roll it on' using two 1–6 dice.

2. Play 'Roll it on' to practise recall of facts for the five- and ten-times tables.

CLOCK FACE 1

OBJECTIVE: to practise facts for the five-times table

LEARNING LINK: kinaesthetic

ORGANISATION: whole class

RESOURCES: a giant clock face drawn on the playground; a beanbag; cardboard clocks and counters (for Now Try This)

WHAT TO DO

● Count in fives as different children step around the giant clock face (see 'Clock face 2' on page 22 in the auditory learning section).

● Use the giant clock face to work out the answer to multiplication questions from the five-times table, for example 2 × 5. Place the beanbag on the number 2. A child stands on number 12 and moves around the clock in a clockwise direction, stepping on each number in turn and counting in fives until they reach the beanbag.

● Repeat for different multiplication calculations. A different child collects the beanbag each time.

NOW TRY THIS

Repeat the activity in the classroom. Use an individual cardboard clock and a counter. Answer a question, for example 6 × 5, by placing the counter on number 6 and then counting around the clock in fives as before.

TARGET BOARD

OBJECTIVE: to begin to derive and recall multiplication facts for the five-times table
LEARNING LINK: kinaesthetic
ORGANISATION: whole class, small groups
RESOURCES: a beanbag or soft ball; a target on the interactive whiteboard or the playground (write a different multiplication question in each section of the target board, for example 4 × 5 or 2 × 5); whiteboards and pens for each child

WHAT TO DO

● One child throws the beanbag at the target and reads out the question that is written in the section of the board that the beanbag hits. (If the beanbag misses the target, someone else tries.)
● In pairs, work out the answer to the question. Record it on your whiteboard.
● Show your answers. Your teacher asks a child to shade in the section of the target board that was hit.
● A different child throws the beanbag, aiming at an unshaded section of the target. Repeat the activity until the whole target board is shaded.

NOW TRY THIS

1. Your teacher writes a different multiple of 5 in each section of the target board, for example 15, 35. Write down a multiplication number sentence that matches the number hit by the beanbag.
2. Play 'Time limit'. Try to play the game and shade in all sections of the target before the time runs out.

FARMYARD STORIES

OBJECTIVE: to improve ability to count in twos; to use the signs × and = to describe and recall a problem
LEARNING LINK: tactile
ORGANISATION: whole class, working in pairs
RESOURCES: a model farm set; whiteboards and pens for each pair

WHAT TO DO

● Listen to the farmyard number story. For example: A farmer has four fields. He puts two cows in each field. How many cows does he have altogether?
● Calculate the answer using the farm set. Create four fields and put two cows in each field. Count the cows in twos to find the answer to the problem. Record this as a number sentence on the board.

● Make up a similar problem. Solve it with a partner. Represent the number story as a picture on your whiteboard. Then solve the problem practically, as a class, using the farm set and record it as a number sentence.

NOW TRY THIS

Make up a number story to match a different calculation, for example, 4 × 5; try using a different theme, such as animals in a zoo.

BAGS OF GOLD

OBJECTIVE: to improve ability to count in fives; to understand multiplication as repeated addition
LEARNING LINK: auditory
ORGANISATION: whole class, small group
RESOURCES: ten laminated moneybags; a dry wipe pen

WHAT TO DO

● There are four money bags on the board. These belong to the giant in the story of Jack and the Beanstalk.
● Every night, after the giant has eaten his dinner, he likes to take out some of his money bags and count the gold coins inside.
● There are five coins in each of the money bags.
● Work out how many coins are in the five money bags altogether. Count in fives, as one child points to each money bag. Say, *4 lots of 5 makes 20.*
● Repeat the activity with a different number of money bags.

NOW TRY THIS

1. Repeat the activity with no visual prompts.
2. The giant has 70 gold coins. He puts 10 pieces of gold in each money bag. How many money bags does he have?

TIMES TABLE JIGSAW

OBJECTIVE: to use the signs × and = to describe and recall a problem; to begin to derive and recall multiplication facts for the five-times table
LEARNING LINK: tactile
ORGANISATION: small groups
RESOURCES: puzzle pieces on small squares of thin card: numbers 1–10, = 5, = 10, = 15, = 20, = 25, = 30, = 35, = 40, = 45, = 50, and ten cards showing × 5 (one set for each group)

WHAT TO DO

● Look at the set of three puzzle pieces on the board and see how they can be matched together to make a calculation from the five-times table. For example: 7 × 5 = 35.
● Suggest other calculations that can be made by matching three of the puzzle pieces together. Continue until all the pieces have been used.
● Work in small groups. Each group shuffles their set of puzzle pieces. Have a race to see which group is the first to correctly organise their cards to make ten complete number sentences from the five-times table.

NOW TRY THIS

1. Complete the same task within a set time.
2. Make a set of puzzle pieces for the ten-times table.

NOAH'S ARK

OBJECTIVE: to understand the operation of multiplication as repeated addition
LEARNING LINK: tactile
ORGANISATION: whole class
RESOURCES: a simple picture book story about Noah's Ark; a toy ark; 20 small-world animal toys (two of each type of animal)

WHAT TO DO

● Listen to the story of Noah's Ark. Remember that Noah took two of each type of creature onto the ark.

● Place two animals of the same type into the ark, for example, two elephants.
● How many groups of animals are in the ark? (1) How many animals are in the ark altogether? (2)
● Put two animals of the same type into the ark. How many groups of animals are in the ark now? (2) How many animals are in the ark altogether? (4)
● Continue adding animals to the ark two by two, until all of the animals are inside.

NOW TRY THIS

1. Write mental calculations in different ways, for example:
2 + 2 + 2 = 6, or 2 × 3 = 6.
2. Investigate simple problems. For example: Noah let two lions, two elephants and two giraffes onto the ark. How many animals were on the ark altogether?

GREETINGS CARDS

OBJECTIVE: to begin to derive and recall multiplication facts for the five-times table
LEARNING LINK: kinaesthetic
ORGANISATION: whole class, small groups
RESOURCES: a selection of old greetings cards: cut the picture on the front in half, write a multiplication question on one half and the corresponding answer on the other half

WHAT TO DO

● Spread the cards out on the floor, picture-side down.
● A child picks up a question card, for example 7 × 5. Work out the answer to the calculation. A child who gives the correct answer locates the card with 35 on it. Put the two pieces of card together to make a complete picture.
● Work together to match up the remaining cards.
● Repeat the activity in small groups.

NOW TRY THIS

1. Time yourselves to see how quickly you can match up all the cards.
2. Play a Christmas version of the game using old Christmas cards.

DOMINOES

OBJECTIVE: to derive and recall addition doubles of all numbers to five
LEARNING LINK: tactile
ORGANISATION: whole class, small groups
RESOURCES: doubles dominoes 1–5, in a bag; a 1–10 number fan for each child

WHAT TO DO

● Look at the double 5 domino on the board. Discuss why this domino is called double 5. Count how many spots are on the domino altogether. Hold up five fingers on each hand to represent the double. Say together, *Double 5 makes 10 altogether.*
● Repeat the activity for all of the other doubles dominoes in the bag.
● Use your number fan. One child takes a domino out of the bag. Use your number fan to show how many spots are on the domino altogether. Count the spots together to check the answer.

NOW TRY THIS

I am thinking of a doubles domino. It has ten spots altogether. How many spots are on each side of the domino?

WHEELS

OBJECTIVE: to understand the operation of multiplication as repeated addition
LEARNING LINK: auditory
ORGANISATION: whole class
RESOURCES: pictures or photographs of the side view of a variety of wheeled vehicles stuck onto cards (for example car, bus, various lorries, car transporter, bike, tank, train)

WHAT TO DO

● Name each vehicle you see on the cards. Say what it is used for. Look closely at the wheels. Discuss how they are the same/different.
● Show how many wheels a car has by holding up the appropriate number of fingers. Why can you only count two wheels on the picture of a car?
● Your teacher writes 2 + 2 on the board: two wheels at the front and two wheels at the back of the car makes four wheels altogether.

● Focus on each of the vehicles. Record the number of wheels on each vehicle in a number sentence on the board.
● Take the picture cards off the board. Match each picture to the correct number sentence.

NOW TRY THIS

1. Use the symbols × and = to record the number of wheels a vehicle has in a number sentence.
2. Draw the side view of a vehicle with ten wheels.

BUS QUEUE

OBJECTIVE: to use × and = to describe and solve a problem
LEARNING LINK: tactile
ORGANISATION: whole class, small groups
RESOURCES: a giant bus stop; small plastic people figures; pencils and paper

WHAT TO DO

● Four volunteers make a queue at the bus stop. Count how many feet are at the bus stop altogether. Remember to count in twos.
● Say together, *4 lots of 2 makes 8.* Record this as a number sentence on the board, using the symbols × and =. Talk about what each number and symbol in the number sentence represents.
● A different number of children stand at the bus stop; repeat the activity.
● Each small group has a set of play people, paper and a pencil. Solve some simple problems and record the answers in number sentences. For example: If six people are waiting at the bus stop, how many feet are there?

NOW TRY THIS

Investigate other problems. For example: There are eight feet at the bus stop. How many people are waiting at the bus stop altogether?

ROLLER COASTER

OBJECTIVE: to understand multiplication as representing an array

LEARNING LINK: tactile

ORGANISATION: whole class; pairs

RESOURCES: cubes; 12 chairs arranged in rows of two; a picture of a roller coaster

WHAT TO DO

● Look at the picture of a roller coaster. Discuss whether anyone has ever been on a roller coaster. What did the roller coaster look like? Did they enjoy the ride?

● Pretend that the chairs are seats in a roller coaster.

How many rows of seats are in the roller coaster?

How many seats are there in each row?

How many seats are there in the roller coaster altogether?

● Two children sit in the front row of seats: one row of two children equals two children altogether.

● Two children sit in the second row of seats. Describe the new array. Continue filling up the seats one row at a time until the roller coaster is full.

● Pairs: Look at the following problem on the board: How many children can ride in a roller coaster with five rows of seats? Calculate the answer using cubes.

NOW TRY THIS

Investigate other problems. For example: How many rows of seats would there be on a roller coaster for 20 people?

COUNTING PATTERNS

OBJECTIVE: to begin to recognise two-digit multiples of two, five or ten

LEARNING LINK: tactile

ORGANISATION: individuals

RESOURCES: a hundred square and coloured crayon for each child

WHAT TO DO

● Each child has a hundred square and a crayon. Count on the square in jumps of 5 to 50. Shade in the appropriate numbers on the hundred square.

● Look closely at the shaded squares and describe the pattern. What do you notice about the shaded numbers? What is the same about all of the numbers in the first column?

● Discuss the word *multiple*. All of the shaded numbers are multiples of 5. Colour the remaining multiples of 5 on your hundred square. Colour in the squares as quickly as you can, using your knowledge of multiples of 5 and number patterns.

● Use your shaded square to practise counting in fives to 100.

NOW TRY THIS

Shade the pattern of twos or tens on a hundred square.

IN THE PICTURE

OBJECTIVE: TO improve ability to count in steps of two, five and ten

LEARNING LINK: auditory

ORGANISATION: small groups

RESOURCES: paper and pencils; photographs of groups of children in the class doing different activities, for example playing, eating lunch, working

WHAT TO DO

● Each group has a different photograph. Use your photograph to answer the questions on the board. In your group, elect a scribe to record the answer to each question:

1. How many children?

2. How many hands?

3. How many toes?

4. How many eyes?

5. How many fingers?

6. How many pairs of shoes?

● Count systematically, making sure nothing is missed out. Discuss how you can answer the questions most efficiently, for example, by counting in twos to calculate the number of hands, or by counting in fives or tens to calculate the number of fingers and toes.

NOW TRY THIS

1. Record each answer as a repeated addition number sentence.

2. Use pictures of popular sports teams or pop groups.

MATCHING

OBJECTIVE: to understand multiplication as representing an array
LEARNING LINK: auditory
ORGANISATION: small groups
RESOURCES: a set of the following cards for each group: 10 white cards showing: 1 × 2 = 2, 2 × 2 = 4, 3 × 2 = 6, 4 × 2 = 8, 5 × 2 = 10, 6 × 2 = 12, 7 × 2 = 14, 8 × 2 = 16, 9 × 2 = 18, 10 × 2 = 20; 10 coloured cards showing the arrays pictured below

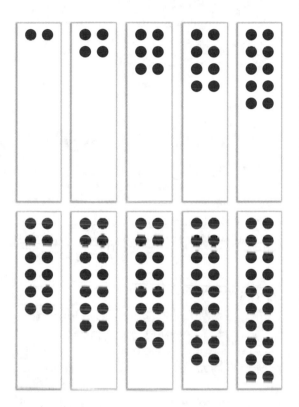

WHAT TO DO

● Each group has a set of cards. Spread the cards out face down on the table.
● Take it in turns to turn over a white card and a coloured card. Describe the array of dots shown on the coloured card, for example, *7 groups of 2 is 14 spots*, and then read out the number sentence on the white card. If the number sentence matches the array, then the cards make a pair and are kept.
● If the cards do not make a pair, they should be turned back over and play passes to the next child.
● The child with the most pairs when all pairs have been correctly matched is the winner.

NOW TRY THIS

1. Each group has a set of number sentence cards. Draw an array of dots to match each number sentence.
2. 'Bar of chocolate' (see page 42 in the tactile learning section).

TEDDY BEARS' PICNIC

OBJECTIVE: to improve ability to count on in steps of two from zero
LEARNING LINK: kinaesthetic
ORGANISATION: whole class, groups
RESOURCES: a set of 11 small, cardboard stepping stones numbered 0, 2, 4, 6, 8, 10, 12, 14, 16, 18, 20; four small teddy bears; a picnic blanket or basket

WHAT TO DO

● Everyone sits in a circle on the floor. The stepping stones are randomly spread out face up in the circle. The picnic basket/blanket and one teddy are next to stepping stone 20. The remaining three bears are on stepping stone 0.
● The three bears want to join their friend on the other side of the river for a picnic. To cross the river safely, the bears must step on the stepping stones in order: 2, 4, 6, 8, and so on.
● Take turns to help move the teddy bears across the stepping stones in the correct order until all of the bears have arrived safely at the picnic site.

NOW TRY THIS

1. Adapt the activity to practise counting in fives and tens.
2. Use a set of giant stepping stones. Pretend to be the teddy bears and step on the stones in the correct order.
3. Help the teddy bears return from their picnic. Move them across the stepping stones from 20 back to zero.

MISSING TENS

OBJECTIVE: to recognise that symbols such as ▲ ■ can be used to stand for an unknown number
LEARNING LINK: tactile
ORGANISATION: whole class, working in pairs.
RESOURCES: paper and pencils; sticks of ten multi-base/interlocking cubes

WHAT TO DO

● Look at the list of ten-times tables facts on the board, each with a missing number. For example:

> $5 \times 10 = ■$
> $▲ \times 10 = 70$

● The different-shaped symbols represent a missing number in each of the number sentences.
● In pairs, identify the missing number in each number sentence.
● Use practical apparatus to help you if necessary.

NOW TRY THIS

Repeat using tables facts for the two- and five-times tables.

PIZZA TOPPINGS

OBJECTIVE: to improve counting in twos, fives and tens; to be able to solve simple mathematical problems
LEARNING LINK: tactile
ORGANISATION: individuals/pairs
RESOURCES: a cardboard pizza with the following toppings: two pieces of pepper, five slices of mushroom, ten pieces of ham (or a representation of this on the interactive whiteboard; paper and pencils for each child

WHAT TO DO

● Look at the pizza. Count how many pieces of each topping are on the pizza.
● Imagine you work in a pizza takeaway. Someone has ordered four pizzas. Work out how many pieces of each topping you would need to make four pizzas exactly the same as the one on the board.

● Write your answer down on a piece of paper.

NOW TRY THIS

1. How many pieces of each topping would you need to make seven pizzas?
2. Design your own pizza and write some simple questions for a partner to solve.

CHRISTMAS CRACKERS

OBJECTIVE: to improve ability to count in tens; to solve simple mathematical problems
LEARNING LINK: tactile
ORGANISATION: individuals/pairs
RESOURCES: a box containing ten Christmas crackers; paper and pencils

WHAT TO DO

● Count how many crackers are in the box.
● You need 50 crackers. How many boxes of crackers do you need to buy?
● How did you work out the answer? Did you remember to count in tens?
● How would you record the mental calculation as a number sentence? ($10 + 10 + 10 + 10 + 10 = 50$)
● Now work out how many boxes of crackers you need to buy to get 100 or 70 crackers. Write a number sentence to show your answer.

NOW TRY THIS

1. You need 75 crackers. How many boxes of crackers do you need to buy? Write a number sentence to show the answer.
2. There are eight boxes of crackers left in the shop. How many crackers altogether?

PLAYING CARDS

OBJECTIVE: to derive and recall doubles of all numbers to ten

LEARNING LINK: auditory

ORGANISATION: whole class

RESOURCES: a pack of giant playing cards with the picture cards removed

WHAT TO DO

- Your teacher holds a pack of playing cards in front of the class. Call out the number that is double the number on the card.
- The class divides into two teams. One child from each team stands up; when your teacher turns over the card at the top of the pack, the first player to double the number on the card correctly scores a point for their team. The team with the most points at the end of the game is the winner.

NOW TRY THIS

1. Play with a time limit. Double the number on as many cards as you can within the time. Play again. Try to beat your previous score.

2. Play the game with a partner using a small pack of playing cards or number cards.

ONE-MINUTE TIME TRIAL

OBJECTIVE: to derive and recall multiplication facts for the two-, five- and ten- times tables

LEARNING LINK: auditory

ORGANISATION: individuals

RESOURCES: a list of 20 multiplication questions for the two-, five- or ten-times tables for each child; pencils; a stopwatch

WHAT TO DO

- Each child has a question sheet and a pencil.
- Answer as many of the questions as you can in one minute.
- Your teacher marks your work.
- Your teacher creates a record of individual scores and the total number of questions answered correctly by the whole class.
- Repeat the 'One minute time trial' on other occasions. Using the same questions, your class tries to beat their previous score each time.

NOW TRY THIS

1. Your teacher reads out (or holds up on flashcards) 20 multiplication questions. Keep up a good pace. Write the answers down.

2. Use a mixed set of questions from the two- and ten-times tables.

RACE TO 100

OBJECTIVE: to derive and recall multiplication facts for the two-, five- or ten-times tables

LEARNING LINK: tactile

ORGANISATION: small groups

RESOURCES: a game board (shade 30 random number squares on a large hundred square); dice; counters; a set of question cards (multiplication questions from the two-, five- or ten-times table) for each group

WHAT TO DO

- Place a coloured counter of your choice on the starting square (number 1 on the game board).
- Take it in turns to roll the dice and move your counter the appropriate number of spaces on the board. If a player lands on a shaded number square, they must turn over a times-table card and try to answer the question on it. If the correct answer is given, the player moves their counter forward three spaces. If a player answers incorrectly, they move their counter back one space.
- The winner is the first player to reach 100.

NOW TRY THIS

Use a mixed set of question cards, including questions from the two-, five- and ten-times tables.

SLEEPING BEAUTY

OBJECTIVE: to derive and recall multiplication facts for the ten-times table
LEARNING LINK: auditory
ORGANISATION: whole class
RESOURCES: two cardboard crowns; ten small cardboard trees with a multiplication calculation from the ten-times table on each

WHAT TO DO

● The trees are arranged in a line across the board. Two children play the roles of the Prince and Sleeping Beauty and stand at opposite ends of the row of trees. Both are wearing a crown.

● The Prince needs to chop down all of the trees in the deep dark forest so that he can rescue Sleeping Beauty. However, an evil fairy has put a spell on the trees. The Prince must answer the question on each tree correctly before he can chop it down.

● One child reads out the calculation on the first tree. Call out the answer to the Prince. The Prince chooses an answer from those called out. If he answers correctly, he can chop the tree down. Repeat until all the questions have been answered correctly and the Prince has rescued Sleeping Beauty.

NOW TRY THIS

1. Use a set of trees with multiplication facts from the two- or five-times table.
2. The Prince has to answer the question on each tree within a time limit.

CHRISTMAS DECORATIONS

OBJECTIVE: to count in twos, fives and tens; to solve simple mathematical problems
LEARNING LINK: tactile
ORGANISATION: individuals/pairs
RESOURCES: a Christmas tree decorated with two bells, five stars and ten baubles

WHAT TO DO

● Look at the Christmas tree. Count how many bells, stars and baubles are on it. How many decorations are on the tree altogether?

● Work out how many bells, stars and baubles you would need to decorate five trees.

● Write your answer on a piece of paper. Explain how you worked the answer out.

NOW TRY THIS

1. How many bells, stars and baubles would you need to decorate ten trees?
2. How many for two trees?
3. Count how many more baubles there are than stars.
4. What number do you need to multiply the number of bells by in order to make the same number of baubles?
5. What number do you need to multiply the number of stars by in order to make the same number of baubles?

BUY ONE GET ONE FREE

OBJECTIVE: to derive and recall doubles of all numbers to at least 10
LEARNING LINK: tactile
ORGANISATION: whole class/small groups
RESOURCES: supermarket carrier bags containing sets of identical objects for example, toilet rolls, tins, chocolate biscuits (there should be an even number of objects in each set)

WHAT TO DO

● There is a special offer on at the supermarket. If you buy a can of pop, you get one free. Yesterday I bought 3 cans of pop. (Place 3 cans on the table.) How many cans did I get free? (Place the remaining 3 cans on the table.) How many cans did I get altogether? (6).

● I bought 7 toilet rolls. (Place 7 toilet rolls on the table.) How many toilet rolls did I get free? (Place the remaining 7 toilet rolls on the table.) How many toilet rolls did I get altogether? (14).

NOW TRY THIS

1. You go to the supermarket. Chocolate bars are on special offer – 'Buy one get one free'. You want 12 chocolate bars altogether. How many do you need to buy?

2. Write some supermarket offer problems for a partner to solve.

DOUBLE DARTS

OBJECTIVE: to derive and recall doubles of all numbers to at least 10
LEARNING LINK: kinaesthetic
ORGANISATION: whole class/small groups
RESOURCES: a toy dartboard and darts; individual whiteboards and pens

WHAT TO DO

● Look at the numbers on the dartboard. Watch me throw the dart. What number have I hit? Double the number to work out how many points I score. Write the answer on your whiteboard.

● Take it in turns to throw a dart at the dartboard. Write down each player's score. Remember to double the number.

NOW TRY THIS

1. You must score 6 points. Which number do you need to hit? (3) Write the answer on your whiteboard.

2. Play 'Double Darts' with two darts. You have to score 16 points. Which 2 numbers could you hit? Write down all the different solutions you can find.

WASHING LINE

OBJECTIVE: to count in fives and begin to recognise multiples of 5
LEARNING LINK: kinaesthetic
ORGANISATION: whole class
RESOURCES: a washing line and pegs; large number cards showing multiples of 5 to 50 or beyond

WHAT TO DO

● Look at the muddled numbers on the washing line. What do you notice about the numbers? Note that they are all multiples of 5 and end in zero or five.

● Peg the smallest number (0) at the beginning of the line. Which number comes next? Continue pegging the numbers out in order until you reach 50.

● Count in unison from 0-50 and back again.

● Close your eyes. Now open them again. Can you work out which number has disappeared?

NOW TRY THIS

1. Two of the numbers on the washing line are in the wrong place. Come and correct the mistake.

2. Play 'Against the Clock'. Try to peg the multiples of five onto the washing line, in order, in less than 1 minute.

TIMES TABLE BINGO

OBJECTIVES: to derive and recall multiplication facts for the two-times table
LEARNING LINK: visual
ORGANISATION: whole class, working individually or in pairs
RESOURCES: a bag containing a set of 1–10 number cards; paper and pencils

WHAT TO DO

- Each child has a piece of paper and a pencil.
- Your teacher writes the even numbers from 2 to 20 randomly on the whiteboard. Pick four of these numbers and write them down.
- Your teacher draws a number card out of the bag, for example 5, and calls out a calculation, for example 5 × 2. If you have written the number 10 on your board, then you may cross it out.
- Remember, if you are not able to recall this number fact from memory, you can use your fingers to calculate the total.
- The winner is the first player to cross out all of their numbers and shout *Bingo*!

NOW TRY THIS

1. Play a different version of the game to practise recall of facts for the five-and ten-times tables.
2. Play the game in groups of three, taking it in turns to be the bingo caller.

SHOUT IT OUT

OBJECTIVES: to begin to derive and recall multiplication facts for the five-times table
LEARNING LINK: kinaesthetic
ORGANISATION: whole class
RESOURCES: a large space, for example, the hall or playground

WHAT TO DO

- The class is divided into four groups. Each group stands in a different corner of the hall or playground.
- You are going to have a competition to find out which group can shout their times tables the loudest.

- One group shouts, *One times five is five*, as loudly as they can. The next group shouts out, *Two times five is ten* as loudly as they can. Continue until a group shouts, *Ten times five is fifty*.
- Decide which group has shouted the loudest. Give them three cheers.

NOW TRY THIS

1. Practise number facts for the two- and ten-times tables in the same way.
2. The whole class stands on one side of the playground opposite the teacher, who shouts out, for example, *Two times two*. Shout back the answer as quickly and loudly as you can.

MUSICAL TIMES TABLES

OBJECTIVES: to derive and recall the multiplication facts for the two-, five- and ten-times tabless
LEARNING LINK: visual
ORGANISATION: whole class
RESOURCES: a cymbal and a beater; number cards; whiteboards and pens

WHAT TO DO

- Look at the multiplication question that your teacher has written on the board, for example, 5 ×10.
- Your teacher will strike the cymbal. When it stops, call out the answer to the calculation.

NOW TRY THIS

1. Practise recalling number facts more quickly by trying to call out the answer before the cymbal stops ringing.
2. Show your answer by holding up a number card or recording it on your whiteboard.

ECHO

OBJECTIVES: to derive and recall multiplication facts for the two-, five- and ten-times tables
LEARNING LINK: kinaesthetic
ORGANISATION: whole class, standing in a circle
RESOURCES: none required

WHAT TO DO

● Watch and then join in with a simple five-beat rhythm, for example tap knees, clap, clap, click fingers. Keep a steady beat as a whole class.
● Your teacher will call out a times table calculation in time with the beat, for example, *One times five is five*. Make an echo by repeating the calculation back in time with the beat.

NOW TRY THIS

Work in small groups. Practise and perform times tables with actions and rhythms you have made up yourselves.

BANG THE DRUM

OBJECTIVES: to begin to learn multiplication facts for the two-times table
LEARNING LINK: visual
ORGANISATION: whole class
RESOURCES: a small drum and beater

WHAT TO DO

● Your teacher writes a multiplication calculation, for example 7 × 2, on the board. Discuss what each number and symbol in the number sentence means. Establish that the answer can be calculated by counting 7 lots of 2.
● Your teacher uses the drum to help you work out what 7 lots of 2 is: it is struck seven times as you count in jumps of two. Record the answer (14) on the board.

● Study the calculation that your teacher has now written, for example 4 × 2. How many lots of 2 do we need to count to calculate the answer? The child who gives the correct answer first can beat the drum to help the class work out the answer.

NOW TRY THIS

Swap the drum for a different percussion instrument and practise facts for the five- and ten-times table.

IN THE BAND

OBJECTIVES: to count in twos; to begin to recognise multiples of two
LEARNING LINK: visual
ORGANISATION: whole class
RESOURCES: a selection of small percussion instruments; number cards showing even numbers 2–20; five chairs

WHAT TO DO

● Five children sit on chairs in a row in front of the class. They choose an instrument to play.
● Your teacher deals each band member two number cards; the numbers are to tell the band members when it is their turn to play their instrument.
● The child who has been dealt the number 2 card plays their instrument first. The children are asked, *Who has the number that is 2 more than 2?* The child who has 4 plays their instrument, followed by whoever has the 6, 8, 10, and so on.
● Swap to a different group of musicians. Once you are familiar with the activity, the band should play their instruments in order without prompting.

NOW TRY THIS

1. Play the game again, but instead of using instruments, perform an action when it is your turn.
2. Practise the activity in groups. Each group could perform to the rest of the class.
3. Play again but with ten children in the band. Each child has just one number card.

CLOCK FACE 2

OBJECTIVES: to improve ability to count in steps of fives

LEARNING LINK: kinaesthetic

ORGANISATION: whole class

RESOURCES: a giant clock face drawn on the playground; number cards of multiples of 5, up to 60

WHAT TO DO

● Remember, there are 60 minutes in an hour and each of the numbers around the clock marks five minutes.

● One volunteer stands on the number 12. They walk around the clock in a clockwise direction, stepping on each of the numbers in order. The whole class counts in fives, each time the volunteer steps on a number.

● Repeat the activity with other volunteers.

NOW TRY THIS

1. Try 'Clock face 1' from the visual learning section (see page 10).

2. Try counting back in fives as the volunteer steps around the clock in an anticlockwise direction.

3. Place number cards showing the multiples of 5, up to 60 in order around the clock face.

LOTTERY

OBJECTIVES: to derive and recall multiplication facts for the ten-times table

LEARNING LINK: visual

ORGANISATION: whole class or small groups

RESOURCES: lottery tickets (small squares of coloured paper); ten ping-pong balls numbered 1–10; a large bowl; stickers or other small rewards

WHAT TO DO

● Your teacher writes the multiples of 10 to 100 on the board and gives each of you a lottery ticket. Choose five numbers from the board and write them on your ticket.

● One child draws one ping-pong ball out of the bowl, for example, the number 7. The child who draws the ball will say, *7 times 10.* If you have written the number 70 on your ticket, cross it out.

● The first player to cross out all the numbers on their ticket and shout *Jackpot!* wins the game.

NOW TRY THIS

1. Try the game again but with different children drawing the lottery numbers.

2. Try using different mathematical language as you play, for example *7 times 10, 7 lots of 10, 7 multiplied by 10,* and so on.

MONEY BOX 1

OBJECTIVES: to improve ability to count in twos, fives or tens

LEARNING LINK: tactile

ORGANISATION: whole class or small groups

RESOURCES: a pot of 2p, 10p or 5p coins; a money box

WHAT TO DO

● Close your eyes. Listen as your teacher drops a handful of 10p coins into the money box slowly, one at a time. How much money is in the money box altogether?

● Your teacher tips the coins out of the moneybox. As a class, count in tens to check the answer.

● Repeat with a different number of coins. Count in your head and use your fingers to keep track of the number of coins that are dropped into the money box.

NOW TRY THIS

1. Use 2p or 5p coins instead of 10p coins, and count in twos or fives.

2. There is 50p in the money box. Can you work out how many coins are in the money box altogether?

MEXICAN WAVE

OBJECTIVES: to improve ability to count on from zero in twos

LEARNING LINK: kinaesthetic

ORGANISATION: whole class

RESOURCES: tape recording of the children counting on from zero in steps of two

WHAT TO DO

● Sit in a circle, on chairs.

● Discuss whether any of you have ever seen a Mexican wave, for example, at football matches or pop concerts. Demonstrate what a Mexican wave looks like, for those children who have never seen one before. Each child in turn quickly stands up, raises their arms in the air and then sits back down.

● Listen to the tape of the class counting in twos. As 2 is chanted, the first child starts the Mexican wave by standing up, lifting their arms in the air and then sitting back down, while shouting out, *Two.* As 4 is chanted, the next child in the circle performs the actions and shouts out, *Four,* and so on.

NOW TRY THIS

Create a Mexican wave while listening to a recording of the class counting in fives or tens.

CARRY ON

OBJECTIVES: to improve ability to count on in twos, fives or tens

LEARNING LINK: visual

ORGANISATION: whole class

RESOURCES: a tape recording of the children counting on from zero in steps of two, five or ten; a small hundred square for each child

WHAT TO DO

● Listen carefully to the number sequence on the tape. Follow the counting pattern on your hundred square.

● When the tape is paused, continue the counting sequence until your teacher gives you a signal to stop.

● Now listen to the rest of the number sequence on the tape. Describe the sequence. Did the numbers increase in steps of two, five or ten?

● Repeat for other number sequences on the tape.

NOW TRY THIS

1. When the tape is paused, write down the next three numbers in the sequence.

2. Listen carefully to the number sequence on the tape. Colour the number pattern on a blank hundred squares.

WHAT'S MISSING?

OBJECTIVES: to improve ability to count on in twos, fives and tens

LEARNING LINK: visual

ORGANISATION: whole class, working in pairs

RESOURCES: a tape recording of a variety of simple number sequences with one number missing, for example 2, 4, 6, _, 10, 12; whiteboards and pens

WHAT TO DO

● Listen to the first sequence of numbers on the tape.

● In pairs, work out the missing number and record it on your whiteboard.

● Hold up your boards on the count of three! Listen to the sequence of numbers again. Watch as the numbers are tracked on a number line and check to see if you have answered correctly.

● Did the numbers in the sequence increase in steps of two, five or ten?

● Play again using another number sequence on the tape.

NOW TRY THIS

1. Identify two or more missing numbers in a longer sequence of numbers.

2. Identify the missing number in a descending sequence of numbers.

AUDITORY LEARNING

HOW OLD?

OBJECTIVES: to solve simple mathematical problems
LEARNING LINK: visual
ORGANISATION: pairs
RESOURCES: paper and pencils

WHAT TO DO

● The following problem is written on the board:

> *Sam is 5.*
> *Sam's brother Joe is 3 times Sam's age.*
> *Dad is 8 times Sam's age.*
> *Grandpa is 12 times Sam's age.*
> *How old is each person in Sam's family?*

● Read the problem as a class. Describe, in your own words, what the problem is asking you to do. What is the key fact that will help you to solve the problem?
● Solve the problem in pairs. (Quick finishers, ask your teacher for a second problem.)
● Gather together as a class. One pair describes how they solved the problem. Do you agree that their answer is correct? How do you know?

NOW TRY THIS

1. Record the answer in a number sentence. For example, Joe is 3 times as old as Sam who is 5. So Joe is 5 + 5 + 5, or 3 × 5.
2. Try other simple logic problems that require you to count in steps of 2, 5 or 10.
3. Make up a problem of your own for a friend to solve.

COUNTING COLLISION

OBJECTIVES: to improve ability to count on in twos and fives from zero; to begin to recognise multiples of two and five
LEARNING LINK: visual
ORGANISATION: whole class, working in pairs
RESOURCES: a class hundred square; paper and pencils

WHAT TO DO

● The following problem is written on the board:

> *If Sam counts in twos and George counts in fives, when will they both reach the same number?*
> *If Sam and George count on to 50, how many numbers will they say that are the same? Write the numbers in a list.*

● Read the first part of the problem together. Decide what it is asking you to find out.
● Work with a partner to solve the first part of the problem. Gather together as a class. Several pairs state what they think the answer is and explain how they solved the problem. Look at the pattern visually on the class hundred square.
● In pairs, solve the second part of the problem. Try to solve it mentally, or use number squares to help you.

NOW TRY THIS

Using blank hundred squares, fill in different number sequences, for example fives and tens. Look carefully and identify which numbers on the hundred square are multiples of both five and ten.

IT'S A KNOCKOUT

OBJECTIVES: to derive and recall multiplication facts for the two-, five- and ten-times tables
LEARNING LINK: kinaesthetic
ORGANISATION: whole class
RESOURCES: stickers or other small rewards

WHAT TO DO

● You are going to play 'It's a knockout'.
● Two contestants stand up and face each other.
● When a multiplication calculation is called out, for example, 3 × 2, the contestants shout out the answer as quickly and loudly as they can. The first child to call out the correct answer is the winner. Their opponent is knocked out of the game and must sit down.
● A small prize is awarded when certain targets are reached, for example, for a contestant who knocks out three opponents in a row.

NOW TRY THIS

Play in teams. One player from each team stands up. The first child to shout out the correct answer to a calculation scores a point for their team. The first team to score ten points wins the game.

GOAL

OBJECTIVES: to derive and recall multiplication facts for the two-, five- and ten-times tables
LEARNING LINK: kinaesthetic
ORGANISATION: whole class, divided into two teams
RESOURCES: 20 cardboard circles (10 red and 10 blue)

WHAT TO DO

● Split into two teams, 'The Blues' and 'The Reds'.
● The aim of the game is to be the first team to score ten goals. Your teacher will draw a large set of goalposts on the board.

● One player from each team takes a shot at the goal: your teacher calls out a multiplication calculation using the two-, five- or ten-times tables, for example 5 × 10, and the first player to shout out the correct answer scores a goal for their team.
● A red or blue ball is stuck inside the goalposts to record which team scores the goal.
● Continue playing until one team has scored ten goals.

NOW TRY THIS

Play the game for other sports, such as rugby or netball.

COLOURFUL COUNTING

OBJECTIVES: to improve ability to count in tens
LEARNING LINK: visual
ORGANISATION: five groups
RESOURCES: five different-coloured cardboard circles

WHAT TO DO

● Your teacher sticks coloured circles on the board and allocates a colour to each group.
● The class counts together in tens as far as possible from 0 to 100 or beyond. When your teacher points to a coloured spot, for example blue, this is a signal for the 'Blues' to take over counting in tens. 'Reds' take over the count when your teacher points to the red spot, and so on.
● Continue until all groups have had several turns.

NOW TRY THIS

Use different categories to distinguish between the groups, such as shapes or animals.

WITH FEELING!

OBJECTIVES: to derive and recall multiplication facts for the two-, five- and ten-times tables
LEARNING LINK: visual
ORGANISATION: whole class
RESOURCES: a list of multiplication calculations for the five-times table written on the board, (1 × 5 = 5 up to 10 × 5 = 50)

WHAT TO DO

● Name some different feelings, for example, anger, sadness, excitement.
● Choose one of the feelings suggested, for example, anger. How would a person look and sound if they were feeling angry?
● Pretend you are angry. Read the calculations on the board together with feeling! Maintain an angry expression and make your voice sound as angry as you can.

NOW TRY THIS

1. When as question is called out, for example 2 × 5, say the answer in a different way, for example in an excited voice.
2. Practise times tables facts at a fast or slow pace, in a loud or quiet voice, and so on.

SWINGING TED

OBJECTIVES: to improve ability to count in fives
LEARNING LINK: visual
ORGANISATION: whole class
RESOURCES: a small teddy tied to a piece of string

WHAT TO DO

● The teddy is dangling in the air and swinging gently from side to side.
● Count in unison in steps of 5 in time with the swinging teddy. Stop counting when the teddy stops swinging.

● Practise this several times. Shorten and lengthen the string that the teddy is swinging on to vary the speed of counting.
● Different children can swing the teddy and lead the count.

NOW TRY THIS

1. Solve simple problems, for example, if the teddy swings four times, what number will we count to? Close your eyes and visualise the teddy swinging four times or lift four fingers to help you calculate the answer.
2. Count in steps of 2 or 10.

GETTING LOUDER/QUIETER

OBJECTIVES: to improve ability to count in twos
LEARNING LINK:
ORGANISATION: whole class
RESOURCES: none required

WHAT TO DO

● Your teacher points at a child, who counts in steps of 2, starting from 2.
● Your teacher points at another child, who joins in with the count. Different children are pointed at until the whole class is counting loudly in unison.
● Your teacher points at a child, and they stop counting. Another child is pointed at, and so on, until just one child is counting quietly.

NOW TRY THIS

1. Count in steps of 5 or 10.
2. Count in twos. Highlight the numbers on a hundred square. What do you notice about the numbers?

LAST ONE STANDING

OBJECTIVES: to improve ability to count in fives; to begin to recognise multiples of five
LEARNING LINK: kinaesthetic
ORGANISATION: whole class
RESOURCES: a number line; beanbag or small class toy

WHAT TO DO

● Highlight the pattern of fives up to 50 on the number line. Discuss what you notice about these numbers. For example, all the numbers end with a 5 or a 0.
● Stand in a circle and play 'Last one standing': pass the beanbag around the circle while, at the same time, counting together up to 50 in steps of five. The child who is holding the beanbag when the number 50 is reached has to sit down. They are now out of the game but keep counting with the rest of the class.
● Continue counting in fives and passing the beanbag around the circle of children who are still standing.
● The child who is the 'last one standing' is the winner.

NOW TRY THIS

1. Predict who will have to sit down at the end of each turn.
2. Use larger totals. For example, the child who is holding the beanbag when 100 is reached should sit down.
3. Play the game counting back in multiples of 2, 5 or 10. The child holding the beanbag, when zero is reached, must sit down.

TIME TRIAL

OBJECTIVES: to derive and recall multiplication facts for the two-, five- and ten- times tables
LEARNING LINK: kinaesthetic
ORGANISATION: whole class, sitting in a circle
RESOURCES: a racetrack, divided into five sections (a simple outline drawn on a large strip of wallpaper is ideal); a toy car; a stopwatch; cards showing assorted multiplication calculations from the two-, five- and ten-times tables

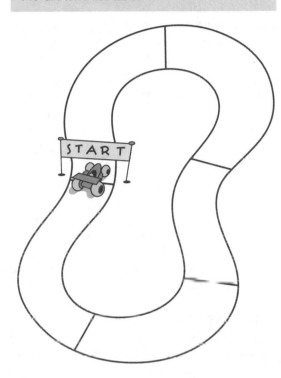

WHAT TO DO

● Sit in a circle, as a class, ready to play 'Time trial'.
● The racetrack is in the centre of the circle with the car on the first section of the track. The cards are shuffled and placed face down in a pile.
● When the stopwatch is started, the top card is turned over and the calculation read out. Call out the answer as quickly as you can. If you answer correctly, move the racing car onto the next section of the track.
● Continue until the car reaches the end of the track. Stop the clock! Record the time it has taken for the racing car to do a complete circuit of the track, on the board.
● Now individual children play 'Time trial'; the times are recorded on the board.

NOW TRY THIS

1. Play 'Time trial' in groups or pairs so that less confident children can join in.
2. Play with two tracks. Have a race, in pairs, to see who can be first to complete a lap of the track.

TIMES TABLE SNAP

OBJECTIVES: to derive and recall multiplication facts for the two-, five- and ten-times tables
LEARNING LINK: kinaesthetic
ORGANISATION: groups of three or four
RESOURCES: a set of number cards showing multiples of 10 from 0 to 100 for each group

WHAT TO DO

● Each group has a set of number cards. Your teacher asks the class a question from the ten-times table, for example 6 × 10. Use your number cards to show the answer. Repeat for other multiplication calculations in the ten-times table.
● Each group selects one number card. Your teacher writes a multiplication calculation on the board, for example 7 × 10. Shout *Snap!* if you think the number you have chosen is the answer to the question and hold up your card.
● A point is awarded to any group holding up the number that is the correct answer to the calculation on the board.
● Continue playing. The group with the most points at the end of the game is the winner.

NOW TRY THIS

Your teacher will give you several sets of calculation and answer cards. Use the cards to play a traditional game of snap.

MONEY BOX 2

OBJECTIVES: to improve ability to count in tens; to understand multiplication as repeated addition
LEARNING LINK: visual
ORGANISATION: whole class, working in pairs
RESOURCES: a money box; 10p coins; whiteboards and pens

WHAT TO DO

● There are six 10p coins in the money box. In pairs, work out how much the coins in the money box are worth altogether.
● Record your answer on your whiteboard. Discuss and compare some of the different strategies that the class used to calculate the answer.

● Tip the coins out of the money box. Count in tens as a class to work out the total value of the coins.
● Repeat the activity with a different number of coins in the money box.

NOW TRY THIS

Solve some simple problems. For example, the total value of the 10p coins in the money box is 80p. How many coins are in the box altogether?

RACE OVER THE MOUNTAIN

OBJECTIVES: to derive and recall number facts for the two-, five- and ten-times tables
LEARNING LINK: tactile
ORGANISATION: whole class, working in small groups
RESOURCES: a whiteboard, dry-wipe pen and a laminated picture of a cartoon character for each group; (draw a mountain on the board and mark three points on each side of the mountain)

WHAT TO DO

● Each group has a cartoon character and sticks it at the base and to the left of the mountain, ready to start the race.
● When your teacher calls out a question from the two-, five- or ten-times table, for example 5 × 2 or 7 × 10, hold up the answer on your whiteboard as quickly as you can. The first group to show the correct answer moves their character one place up the mountain.
● Continue answering multiplication questions until one group has won, by climbing to the top of the mountain and back down the other side.

NOW TRY THIS

Race a friend over the mountain. Use small photos of yourselves as playing pieces. When you answer a calculation correctly, you move one step up the hill; if you answer incorrectly, you move back one step.

TREASURE HUNT

OBJECTIVES: to derive and recall multiplication facts for the two-times table
LEARNING LINK: visual, kinaesthetic
ORGANISATION: whole class or small groups
RESOURCES: a giant five-by-four grid drawn on the playground with chalk (or use masking tape to mark a grid on the hall floor); 20 plastic cups; treasure; two sets of number cards showing multiples of 2 up to 20

WHAT TO DO

● There is a number card and an upturned cup in each section of the grid.
● Underneath some of the cups there is treasure. If you find it, you can keep it.
● When your teacher calls out a multiplication calculation from the two-times table, for example 4 × 2, put up your hand if you know the answer.
● One child answers the question. If they answer correctly, they must find a square on the grid with that number in it (8) and turn the cup over to see if they have found any treasure.
● Continue until all the treasure has been found.

NOW TRY THIS

1. Hunt for a favourite class toy that is hidden under one of the cups.
2. Play in two teams: let Team A hide some treasure for Team B to find, then swap over.

DOUBLES RHYME

OBJECTIVES: to derive and recall addition doubles facts of all numbers up to five
LEARNING LINK: tactile
ORGANISATION: whole class
RESOURCES: none required

WHAT TO DO

● Practise the following action rhyme as a class to help you learn by heart addition doubles facts for numbers up to 5:

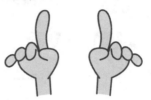

Double 1 makes 2
Hello, how do you do?

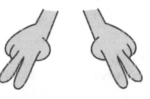

Double 2 makes 4
Now point to the floor.

Double 3 makes 6
Lollipops to lick.

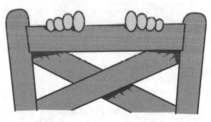

Double 4 makes 8
Open up the gate

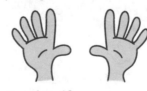

Double 5 makes 10
Wave goodbye and start again

NOW TRY THIS

Devise additional lines and actions for the poem to help you remember addition doubles up to 10 + 10.

POCKET MONEY

OBJECTIVE: to understand multiplication as repeated addition
LEARNING LINK: visual
ORGANISATION: whole class, working in pairs
RESOURCES: a pot of 10p pieces and a cardboard piggy bank for each pair

WHAT TO DO

● Working in pairs, put four 10p coins into your piggy bank.
● Calculate how much money is in your piggy bank altogether.
● Demonstrate how you calculated the answer by counting in tens. Remember, 4 lots of 10p is 40p.
● Repeat the activity several times with different amounts of money.
● Next, take it in turns to tell your partner how many coins to put in the piggy bank. Calculate the total amount.
● If you need to, refer to a hundred square with the tens column highlighted.

NOW TRY THIS

1. Repeat the activity using 2p or 5p pieces.
2. Work out how many 10p coins are in the piggy bank when given a total, for example 80p.
3. Set up a small shop in the classroom with all items priced as multiples of 10p. Take it in turns to buy an item, counting out how many 10p coins you need.

PARKING TICKET

OBJECTIVE: to improve ability to count in tens; to solve simple problems
LEARNING LINK: visual
ORGANISATION: whole class, working in groups of two or three
RESOURCES: a pot of 10p coins per group; a simple car-park ticket machine made out of an empty cereal box

WHAT TO DO

● Look at the car park ticket machine. The only coins that can be used in this ticket machine are 10p pieces.
● Listen to a simple story. For example: *Mr Green parked his car in the car park while he went shopping. When he got back to the car park and put his ticket into the machine, it told him that he must pay 70p. How many coins did he need to put into the machine?*
● Each group has a pot of 10p coins. Use the coins to help you work out the answer to Mr Green's problem.
● One group comes to the front and explains their strategy. One member of the group pretends to be Mr Green. They put the correct money into the machine, one coin at a time (70p). The class count in tens to check that the correct amount is paid.
● Repeat the activity using a different number story.

NOW TRY THIS

1. Represent the transaction with a number sentence, for example. 7 × 10p = 70p.
2. Adapt the ticket machine so that it only takes 5p or 2p coins.
3. Mr Black puts four 10p coins into the ticket machine. How much did he pay?

WASH DAY

OBJECTIVE: to improve ability to count in twos
LEARNING LINK: visual
ORGANISATION: whole class, pairs
RESOURCES: a classroom washing line; several pairs of socks in a basket; pegs

WHAT TO DO

● Look at one basket of socks. How many socks are there in a pair?
● Different children come to the front and locate a pair of socks in the basket. Count how many pairs of socks were in the basket altogether. Return all the socks to the basket.
● In pairs, work together to calculate how many pegs you would need to hang out all the pairs of socks onto the washing line.
● Different pairs share the strategy they used to work out the answer with the rest of the class.
● One pair pegs the socks onto the washing line. Count the number of pegs out loud to check that you have solved the problem correctly.

NOW TRY THIS

1. Repeat the activity with a different number of pairs of socks, or gloves.
2. Write a number sentence which shows how you calculated the number of pegs needed to hang out the pairs of socks, for example $7 \times 2 = 14$.

THREADING RACE

OBJECTIVE: to improve ability to count in fives
LEARNING LINK: auditory
ORGANISATION: groups of three or four
RESOURCES: string; a pot of threading objects for each group – for example, pasta tubes, cotton reels, beads, buttons; a stopwatch

WHAT TO DO

● You are going to have a threading competition.
● Each group has a length of string and a pot of things to thread. Nominate a 'threader' from each group to take part in the first 'Threading race'. The 'threader' threads as many things as they can onto their string in one minute. Five points will be awarded for each item they manage to thread.
● At the end of the race, calculate your score by counting in fives.
● The group that achieves the highest score is awarded a point.
● Repeat the activity several times until everybody has been 'threader' participated in at least one 'Threading race'.

NOW TRY THIS

Have a tower-building race using interlocking cubes. Score two or ten points for each cube in the tower.

COVER UP

OBJECTIVE: to derive and recall multiplication facts for the ten-times table
LEARNING LINK: visual
ORGANISATION: whole class; pairs
RESOURCES: two number strips marked with the multiples of 10 up to 100, a set of 1–10 number cards and 20 counters for each pair

WHAT TO DO

● Look at the number strip. What do you notice about the numbers? Note that they are all multiples of 10 and end in zero. Count in unison from 0 to 100 and back.
● Play 'Cover up' in pairs: shuffle a set of number cards and place them face down on the table. Turn over the top card and multiply the number on the card by ten. Cover that number on the number strip with a counter.
● The aim of the game is to be the first player to cover up all the numbers on their number strip. (Once the number cards have all been turned over once, shuffle the pack and begin again.)

NOW TRY THIS

1. Adapt the game to practise times-table facts for the two- and five-times tables.
2. Play 'Cover up' as a whole-class activity in two teams.

AT THE FAIR

OBJECTIVE: to improve ability to count in fives
LEARNING LINK: auditory
ORGANISATION: whole class, working in pairs
RESOURCES: a picture of a fairground ride, for example, a big wheel or dodgems; a laminated purse or wallet and ten 5p coins per pair

WHAT TO DO

● Each pair has a purse and ten coins to place on it. Count how much money you have altogether. Several different children model to the rest of the class how they counted in fives to find the total.
● Look at the picture of a fairground ride displayed on the board. It costs 5p to have one go on the ride.
● Now listen to a number story, such as: *Sam went to the fair. He had seven goes on the big wheel. How much money did he spend?*
● If necessary, use the coins in the purse to calculate the answer to the problem practically.
● Repeat for other number stories.

NOW TRY THIS

1. Make up your own number stories for a partner to solve.
2. Repeat the activity in a different context, for example, a sweet shop.

SHOPPING

OBJECTIVE: to improve ability to count in tens; to understand the operation of multiplication as repeated addition
LEARNING LINK: auditory
ORGANISATION: whole class
RESOURCES: a selection of small items all priced at a multiple of 10p; a purse filled with 10p coins

WHAT TO DO

● Arrange the priced items on a table at the front of the class. The shopkeeper (your teacher) shows you what is for sale in the shop. In this shop, the customer may only pay with 10p coins.

● One child comes and buys something from the shop. They must count out the correct number of coins to pay from the purse.
● The shopkeeper checks the customer has given the correct amount of money by counting in tens. Remember, multiplication is repeated addition: 6 lots of 10p makes 60p, and so on.
● Different children come and buy something from the shop. When you are not buying, anticipate the number of coins the customer needs to pay, by counting on your fingers.

NOW TRY THIS

1. Adjust the price of the items in the shop so that the customers pay in 5p or 2p pieces.
2. Work out which item a customer bought from the number of coins the shopkeeper has collected.

HELPING HANDS

OBJECTIVE: to improve ability to count in twos; to begin to learn multiplication facts for the two-times-table
LEARNING LINK: auditory
ORGANISATION: whole class
RESOURCES: none required

WHAT TO DO

● Imagine that each of your fingers is worth 2. Lift each finger in turn while counting in twos to 20.
● Practise counting in unison in this way as a class. Make sure that you raise one finger each time that you count on another two.
● Count to 6 in twos. How many twos make 6? Notice that the answer is the number of fingers that you are holding up.
● Count in twos to other even numbers, for example 14 or 18. Each time the target number is reached, answer the question: How many twos make _? Remember to count your raised fingers to find out the answer.

NOW TRY THIS

1. Use your 'helping hands' to count in fives and tens.
2. Use your 'helping hands' to calculate the answers to multiplication questions.

GRABBING CONTEST

OBJECTIVE: to improve ability to count in twos
LEARNING LINK: visual
ORGANISATION: whole class or groups
RESOURCES: a large pair of gardening gloves; a tray of small plastic shapes such as cubes, bears or beads

WHAT TO DO

● A tray of objects is on a table at the front of the class. You are going to take part in a 'Grabbing contest'. A volunteer is chosen to 'grab' first. They come out to the front and put on the 'grabbing gloves'.

● The 'grabber' picks up as many of the objects on the tray as they can in one go. They will be awarded two points for each object they grab. The grabber calculates the score by counting in twos.

● The class helps to check that the score has been calculated correctly by counting in twos in unison.

● Take it in turns to be the 'grabber'. Record your scores in a simple table (see below). At the end of the game, the player with the highest score is the winner.

Name	Number of items grabbed	Score

NOW TRY THIS

1. Use the results in the table to answer questions such as: how many twos make 12?
2. Try to calculate your score by recalling the appropriate multiplication fact. For example: how many cubes did you grab? (8) What are 8 lots of 2?
3. Investigate how many beads you would need to grab to achieve a particular score.

HOW MANY CAN YOU BUY?

OBJECTIVE: to improve ability to count in twos; to solve simple mathematical problems
LEARNING LINK: visual
ORGANISATION: pairs
RESOURCES: ten identical objects in a container, for example, sweets, toy cars, pencils; a set of ten cubes and pot of ten 2p pieces for each pair

WHAT TO DO

● At the front of the class is a box of sweets. Each sweet costs 2p.

● Listen to a number story about one of the children in the class. For example: *Joanne went to the sweet shop. She spent 16p. How many sweets did she buy?*

● In pairs, work out the answer using a pot of 2p coins and a set of cubes (sweets). Show your answer by holding up the appropriate amount of cubes.

● Discuss the strategies that have been used to work out the answer. Try solving the problem in the following way: count out 16p in 2p pieces and match a sweet to each 2p. Because there are 8 twos in 16, Joanne is able to buy 8 sweets.

● Solve other similar problems. Try to solve the problems without practical apparatus.

NOW TRY THIS

1. Set simple problems for your partner to solve.
2. Represent your number story as a number sentence.
3. Set up a simple shop in the classroom where children must pay for items using 2p, 5p or 10p coins only.

ROLL IT!

OBJECTIVE: to begin to know multiplication facts for the two-times table
LEARNING LINK: visual
ORGANISATION: whole class, working in pairs
RESOURCES: photocopiable page 60 'Roll it!' gameboard, a 1–6 dice and two sets of different-coloured counters for each pair

WHAT TO DO

● Play 'Roll it!' in pairs. One of you rolls the dice and multiplies the number rolled by 2. You then cover the total on the board with one of your counters.

● Take it in turns to play until all of the numbers have been covered. If a player makes a number, for example 4, and all the fours on the board are already covered, they must miss a turn. The winner is the player with the most counters on the board at the end of the game.

NOW TRY THIS

1. Practise recall of other facts in the two-times table: play with a gameboard that includes all even numbers to 20. Take it in turns to select a 1–10 number card and multiply the number by two.
2. Adapt the game to practise facts for other times tables.

AT THE POST OFFICE

OBJECTIVE: to improve ability to count in twos, fives or tens; to understand multiplication as repeated addition
LEARNING LINK: visual
ORGANISATION: whole class; pairs
RESOURCES: a set of 2p, 5p or 10p stamps for each pair; a sack of parcels or letters for posting; scales

WHAT TO DO

● One child picks a parcel out of the sack and brings it to the post office.
● The cashier (your teacher) weighs the parcel on the scales. It needs 30p worth of stamps to send it.

● In pairs, work out how many stamps you need to send the parcel, using a set of 5p stamps.
● The cashier sticks six stamps on the parcel and says, *6 lots of 5p make 30p altogether.*
● Repeat the activity until the sack of parcels is empty.

NOW TRY THIS

Solve simple problems, using a set of 2p, 5p and 10p stamps. For example: make 20p using stamps of the same value. How many ways of making 20p are there? (10×2, 4×5, 2×10)

BEAD STRINGS

OBJECTIVE: to improve ability to count in twos; to understand the operation of multiplication as repeated addition
LEARNING LINK: visual
ORGANISATION: whole class
RESOURCES: a giant bead string of 20 beads (the beads should alternate in colour in groups of two, for example two red, two blue, two red and so on); smaller bead strings for the children to use; a list of even numbers up to 20 written on the board

WHAT TO DO

● Group all of the beads together at one end of the giant string. What do you notice about the beads? (They are grouped in twos; there are 20 beads altogether.)

● Count in twos in unison as one child slides the beads, two by two, to the opposite end of the string.

● One child moves 8 beads (in groups of two) to the other end of the string. How many groups of two make 8? This is clearly illustrated by the different-coloured beads.

● Repeat this activity for other numbers up to 20.

● Use your bead strings to work out how many groups of two are in a list of numbers written on the board.

NOW TRY THIS

Repeat the activity using towers of interlocking cubes instead of bead strings.

QUEEN OF HEARTS

OBJECTIVE: to understand multiplication as representing an array
LEARNING LINK: visual
ORGANISATION: small groups
RESOURCES: an apron with a large heart shape pinned on the front; 50 small cardboard heart shapes and 30 heart shapes stuck onto an oven tray in an array six by five for each group

WHAT TO DO

● Your teacher is wearing the apron and holding up the tray of tarts. Who is your teacher pretending to be? Sing the nursery rhyme together.
● The Queen of Hearts bakes a fresh batch of tarts every day. She always lays the tarts out in rows of five so that if anyone pinches one, she will notice straight away.
● Discuss the arrangement of the tarts on the tray. Make sure that there are six rows, each containing five tarts.
● In your group, copy the arrangement of tarts, using a set of cardboard hearts, and count how many tarts there are altogether.
● Use your cardboard hearts to investigate how you would lay out 20 tarts on a tray. Remember, the Queen of Hearts always lays her tarts out in rows of five. Repeat for other multiples of 5.

NOW TRY THIS

Draw 25 tarts on a tray and then use the symbols × and = to record the calculation in a number sentence.

ROCKETS

OBJECTIVE: to improve ability to count in fives; to understand multiplication as repeated addition
LEARNING LINK: visual
ORGANISATION: whole class
RESOURCES: several rocket fireworks drawn on the board, each with five stars exploding out of the top

WHAT TO DO

● Look at the fireworks on the board. How many rockets are there? How many stars are coming out of each rocket? How many stars are there altogether? Remember to count in fives.
● Pretend that your arm is a rocket. Clench your fist by your side and then shoot your arm into the air and explode five fingers to represent five stars.
● Different-sized groups of children come out to the front and create firework displays by taking it in turns to launch an exploding rocket. The rest of the class should count the stars in fives (each rocket has five stars). Remember, multiplication is repeated addition, for example 5 + 5 + 5 + 5 makes 20 stars.

NOW TRY THIS

1. Represent each firework display as a number sentence.
2. Solve some number problems in pairs. For example:
5 rockets = ___ stars
7 rockets = ___ stars
10 rockets = ___ stars

5p EXCHANGE

OBJECTIVE: to improve ability to count in fives; to understand the operation of multiplication as repeated addition
LEARNING LINK: visual
ORGANISATION: groups of two or three
RESOURCES: a pot of 1p, 5p, and 50p pieces (toy money) and a 1–3 dice or spinner for each group

WHAT TO DO

● Each group has a pot of coins and a dice. Take it in turns to roll the dice and collect that number of pennies. As soon as you have collected five pennies, exchange them for a 5p piece. You can carry forward any remaining 1p coins to your next turn.
● Continue taking it in turns to collect and exchange pennies for 5p coins until one member of the group has collected ten 5p coins. Count the ten 5p coins: if you do this correctly, exchange the coins for a 50p piece. The winner is the child who has collected the most 50p pieces at the end of the game.

NOW TRY THIS

Use a 1–6 dice. Collect ten pennies and then exchange them for a 10p piece. Exchange ten 10p pieces for a £1 coin.

FINGER DOUBLES

OBJECTIVE: to recall the doubles of all numbers to ten
LEARNING LINK: visual
ORGANISATION: whole class
RESOURCES: none required

WHAT TO DO

● Two children come out to the front. Both hold up three fingers. Count how many fingers the children are holding up altogether. Remember, when two numbers the same are put together it is called a double. Say, *Double 3 makes 6 altogether*.
● Everyone holds up five fingers. Find a partner and hold your fingers side by side to show double 5. Say, *Double 5 makes 10 altogether*.
● Practise doubling other numbers up to ten.

NOW TRY THIS

Double numbers between one and ten as they are pointed at on the board. Shout out the answer as quickly as you can.

ROLL THE BUTTONS

OBJECTIVE: to improve ability to count in twos, fives and tens; to derive and recall multiplication facts for the two-, five- and ten-times-tables
LEARNING LINK: visual
ORGANISATION: groups of three or four
RESOURCES: a large sheet of sugar paper divided into three numbered sections (see below) and a pot of ten buttons (or coins or counters) for each group

WHAT TO DO

● Play 'Roll the buttons': the numbers on the gameboard show how many points a player will score for each button that lands in that section of the board.
● Roll ten buttons onto the board and calculate how many points have been scored: count how many counters have landed within the ten-point section of the board. Multiply that number by ten. Repeat for the counters in the other sections of the board. Add the three amounts together to find the total score.

● Play the game in small groups. The player who achieves the highest score is the winner.

NOW TRY THIS

You could try a simpler version of the game with only one target area. Any buttons that land outside of the target do not score.

POSTBOX

OBJECTIVE: to begin to recognise two-digit multiples of two, five and ten
LEARNING LINK: visual
ORGANISATION: whole class
RESOURCES: four cardboard post boxes labelled 'Multiples of 2', 'Multiples of 5', 'Multiples of 10', 'Other Numbers'; a sack of envelopes, each with a two-digit number clearly marked on the front

WHAT TO DO

● Count in multiples of 2, 5 and 10 from 0.
● One child picks a letter out of the sack and decides which post box they think the letter should be posted in. The rest of the class checks to see if this is correct by counting.
● Remember, some numbers can be multiples of 2, 5 *and* 10 and so many of the letters can be posted in more than one of the post boxes.

NOW TRY THIS

1. Investigate which numbers are multiples of 2, 5 and 10.
2. Write a three-digit number on each envelope to make the activity more challenging.

WINTER WARMERS

OBJECTIVE: to understand the operation of multiplication as repeated addition; to practise counting in twos
LEARNING LINK: visual
ORGANISATION: whole class
RESOURCES: a bag of woolly gloves and socks; a washing line; bag of pegs

WHAT TO DO

● How many gloves, shoes or socks make a pair?
● How many gloves are there in three pairs? Several children share their answer with the class.
● One child takes three pairs of gloves out of the basket and pegs them on the washing line. Count the gloves in twos. Point to each pair of gloves in turn and say, *2 + 2 + 2 = 6 gloves altogether*.
● Repeat, changing the number of pairs of socks or gloves each time. For example, how many socks are there in six pairs, or five pairs? A different child pegs out the appropriate number of pairs of gloves or socks on the line each time to check the answer.

NOW TRY THIS

How many shoes do you need for seven children to each have a pair to wear?

FOOTPRINTS IN THE SNOW

OBJECTIVE: to understand the operation of multiplication as repeated addition
LEARNING LINK: visual
ORGANISATION: groups of three or four
RESOURCES: play dough (add some glitter to the dough for extra sparkle); small plastic figures; paper; pencils

WHAT TO DO

● Look at the ball of sparkly dough that your teacher has rolled out to represent snow. A plastic figure has been pushed into the dough to make two footprints.
● Listen to a simple story: *Sunita was playing in the snow. She jumped from one side of her garden to the other. She made five big jumps. How many footprints did she leave in the snow?*

● Each group has a ball of dough and a plastic figure to help them solve the problem practically. How many jumps did Sunita make? How many footprints were left by each jump? How many footprints were left altogether? Record the calculation as a number sentence, for example 2 + 2 + 2 + 2 + 2 = 10.
● Repeat the activity for other number stories.

NOW TRY THIS

Write number sentences to describe the rectangular arrays created by pushing different-sized bricks into wet sand or dough.

TEDDY TRAIN

OBJECTIVE: to practise counting in twos; to be able to solve mathematical problems
LEARNING LINK: visual
ORGANISATION: groups
RESOURCES: a set of small teddy bears; a 'Teddy train' with six carriages, made from a model train engine and empty match boxes

WHAT TO DO

● At the front of the class is a 'Teddy train' with six carriages. Two teddies can travel in each carriage.
● Work out how many bears would be able to travel on this train altogether. Try different strategies to work out the answer. For example, hold up six fingers and count them in twos.
● Put two bears in each carriage until the train is full. Count in twos to see how many bears are on the train altogether.
● Solve other problems, for example, how many bears can travel on a train with five carriages, or four carriages?

NOW TRY THIS

1. Investigate how many carriages would be required to carry a specified number of bears.
2. Solve similar problems where five bears can travel in each carriage.

MAKE A FACE

OBJECTIVE: to recall addition doubles of all numbers to six
LEARNING LINK: visual
ORGANISATION: groups of two to four
RESOURCES: photocopiable page 61: Make a face, paper and pencils and a 1–6 dice for each group

WHAT TO DO

● Play 'Make a face'. The aim of the game is to be the first person to draw a face with two eyes, two ears, a nose, a mouth and some hair.
● Take it in turns to roll the dice, double the number of spots shown and then look on the game card to see which facial feature you can draw. For example, if you roll 3, you can draw a nose (6).
● You must score 12 and draw a face first, before you can begin to collect the remaining facial features.

NOW TRY THIS

1. Hold a doubles beetle drive.
2. Use a spinner labelled 1×2, 2×2, 3×2, 4×2, 5×2, 6×2 instead of a dice.

COUNTING

OBJECTIVE: to practise counting in twos, fives and tens
LEARNING LINK: visual
ORGANISATION: whole class; small groups
RESOURCES: several small plastic bowls containing dried pasta shapes dyed with brightly coloured food colouring

WHAT TO DO

● Sit in a circle. Pass the bowl filled with coloured pasta shapes around the circle. When it gets to you, estimate how many pieces of pasta are in the bowl altogether.
● Can you think of a way to count the total number of pasta shapes quickly and efficiently? For example, by arranging the pasta shapes into groups of two, five or ten.

● Different children help group the pasta into sets of two. Count in twos to calculate how many pieces of pasta there are altogether.
● Different children group and count the pasta in fives and tens.
● Work in groups. Each group has a bowl of pasta shapes. Estimate the number. Then count the shapes by arranging the pasta into groups of two, five and then ten.

NOW TRY THIS

Count sweets in a jar or chocolates in a tin in the same way.

BEANS

OBJECTIVE: to begin to recognise multiples of 5 and 10
LEARNING LINK: visual
ORGANISATION: whole class; pairs
RESOURCES: photocopiable page 62: Beans, and a pot of dried beans for each pair; an enlarged version of the photocopiable page for whole-class use

WHAT TO DO

● There is a pile of 30 beans on the table. Remember how to group and count in ones, fives and tens. As a class, fill in the information gathered on an enlarged copy of the recording sheet.
● Each group has a pot of beans and a recording sheet. Use the beans to investigate which of the numbers can be grouped into piles of five and ten.
● Discuss the information that has been gathered as a class. What do you notice about all the numbers that can be grouped into fives and tens? Do you think number 13 is a multiple of five or ten? Why not?

NOW TRY THIS

1. Investigate a different set of numbers to find out whether they are multiples of 2, 10 or both.
2. Apply your knowledge of multiples to predict whether a particular number is a multiple of five or ten. Then use practical apparatus to check your answer.

LEAP FROG

OBJECTIVE: to practise counting in twos; to understand multiplication as repeated addition
LEARNING LINK: visual
ORGANISATION: whole class
RESOURCES: a frog finger puppet or counter; a number line or hundred square

WHAT TO DO

● Count in twos as the frog hops along the number line. Predict: Will the frog land on 18? Will the frog land on 15? How do you know?
● Count to different numbers. Use your fingers to keep a tally of how many jumps the frog makes each time.
● Solve some simple problems. For example: The frog starts at 0. It makes 6 hops of 2. What number will the frog land on?
● Count on your fingers to calculate the answer as quickly as you can.

NOW TRY THIS

1. Practise division. Predict how many hops of 2 the frog needs to make to reach a target number.
2. Recite the two-times table up to 10 × 2. Hold up a finger to represent each two counted.

LEAP FROG 2

OBJECTIVE: to practise counting in twos, fives and tens; to understand multiplication as repeated addition
LEARNING LINK: visual
ORGANISATION: groups of three or four
RESOURCES: a frog finger puppet or counter; a 0–100 number line; a spinner with numbers 2, 5 and 10; a 1–6 dice; a sheet of blank number lines and a green counter for each group; a blank number line on the board

WHAT TO DO

● Chant in twos, fives and tens as the frog hops along the number line.
● One child spins the spinner to determine the size of hop the frog will make and rolls the dice to decide how many hops the frog will make.

+10 +10 +10 +10

```
0    10   20   30   40   50   60
```

● Add the frog hops to the number line on the board. For example, if the spinner lands on 10 and a six is rolled on the dice, the number line should look like the one above.
● Each group has a dice, a spinner, a sheet of blank number lines and a frog counter. Create some frog number lines of your own.

NOW TRY THIS

1. Use a 1–9 dice to make the activity more challenging.
2. Write a number sentence below each number line (for example: 10 + 10 + 10 + 10 + 10 + 10 = 60).

FIVE-POINTED STARS

OBJECTIVE: to improve ability to count in fives; to begin to derive and recall multiplication facts for the five-times table
LEARNING LINK: visual
ORGANISATION: groups of three or four
RESOURCES: small wooden lollipop sticks or thin strips of card; paper and pencils

WHAT TO DO

● Your teacher demonstrates how to make a five-pointed star by overlapping five lollipop sticks.
● Each group has a set of lollipop sticks. Investigate how many sticks are needed to make different numbers of stars.
● Come together as a class and write a simple results table on the board.

Number of stars	Number of sticks	Total number of sticks
1	1 x 5	5
2	2 x 5	10

NOW TRY THIS

1. Glue and glitter the stars to make an attractive classroom display.
2. Use a set of pentagons. Find the total number of sides by counting in fives.

GETTING READY FOR WINTER

OBJECTIVE: to begin to derive and recall multiplication facts for the two times table; to use × and = signs to record mental calculations in a number sentence
LEARNING LINK: visual
ORGANISATION: whole class; pairs
RESOURCES: a big bag of acorns and/or cubes to represent acorns

WHAT TO DO

● As a class, talk about how squirrels get ready for winter. What do they eat? How do they make sure they have enough food to last them through the winter?
● Listen to a simple story. *On Friday, Cyril the squirrel collected some acorns. He buried the acorns in the ground to keep them safe through the winter. Cyril dug nine holes. He put two acorns in each hole. How many acorns did he bury altogether?*
● Each pair has a pile of acorns or cubes to work with. Work out the answer by acting out the story.
● One pair demonstrate how they worked out the answer by grouping the acorns in twos. Say together, *9 lots of 2 equals 18*. Record the calculation as a number sentence on the board.

NOW TRY THIS

1. Tell the story again, but change the number of holes. Calculate the answer to the problem in pairs and record the calculation as a number sentence.
2. Practise division by working out how many holes the squirrel would need to dig to bury (for example) eight acorns.

PEGBOARDS

OBJECTIVE: to understand multiplication as representing an array
LEARNING LINK: visual
ORGANISATION: pairs
RESOURCES: pegboards and pegs

WHAT TO DO

● Your teacher has made an array using 6 lots of 2 pegs.

● Describe the array you can see. Use a range of language. For example, *6 sets of 2, 6 groups of 2, 6 rows of 2*. Count in twos to find the total number of pegs.
● Each pair has an even number of pegs up to 20. Arrange the pegs in groups of two to make a simple array.
● Each pair describes the array they have created to the rest of the group.

NOW TRY THIS

Practise making and naming arrays using cubes, counters, squared paper, and so on.

SPEEDY SHOW ME

OBJECTIVE: to practise selected times-table facts
LEARNING LINK: auditory
ORGANISATION: individuals
RESOURCES: a set of cards with the answers to selected two-times table facts on them, for example 1 × 2, 2 × 2, 3 × 2, for each child

WHAT TO DO

● Look at your set of number cards.
● Your teacher calls out a calculation, for example 1 × 2. Show the answer by holding up the correct number card. Discuss the different strategies that different children have used to calculate the answer, for example, counting on the number line or using fingers. Repeat for each of the calculations.
● Play 'Speedy show me'. Your teacher calls out the calculations in any order. Hold up the correct answer as quickly as you can.
● The pace of questioning will gradually increase.

NOW TRY THIS

Write your answer to each question on your whiteboard.

COLOUR BY NUMBERS

OBJECTIVE: to begin to recognise multiples of five
LEARNING LINK: visual
ORGANISATION: Individual
RESOURCES: a giant hundred square; a simple colouring picture or pattern for every child (write a different number in each section of the picture); colouring pencils

WHAT TO DO

● Count in fives. Your teacher highlights the number sequence on a large hundred square. What do you notice about the highlighted numbers? Remember that these numbers, all of which end with 0 or 5, are called multiples of 5.

● Each child has a colouring sheet and two coloured crayons.

● Look at the following instructions on the board:

Colour numbers that are a multiple of 5 red.	Colour numbers that are not a multiple of 5 blue.

● Colour each section of your picture red or blue according to whether the number inside it is/is not a multiple of five.

NOW TRY THIS

This time there is a simple multiplication calculation in each section of the picture. Your teacher has written a simple colour key on the board. For example: 10 – red, 20 – blue 15 – pink and so on. Work out the answer to each question and colour the picture using the right colours.

COLOURING ARRAYS

OBJECTIVE: to understand multiplication as representing an array
LEARNING LINK: visual
ORGANISATION: whole class, working individually
RESOURCES: a sheet of squared paper and a coloured crayon for each child; an enlarged sheet of squared paper for demonstration

WHAT TO DO

● Look at the list of even numbers on the board, for example 6, 8, 10, 12, 16.

● One child chooses a number from the board, for example 8. Your teacher demonstrates how to colour in four groups of two squares to make an array, and models how to write this as a multiplication calculation (4 × 2).

● Each child has a piece of squared paper and a crayon. Colour in a multiplication array to match each of the numbers on the board.

NOW TRY THIS

1. Write the corresponding multiplication calculation beside each array

2. Repeat the activity using multiples of 5 or 10.

FIVE-TIMES TABLE FACTS

OBJECTIVE: to begin to know by heart multiplication facts for the five-times table
LEARNING LINK: visual
ORGANISATION: pairs
RESOURCES: a set of number cards showing multiples of 5 (up to 50) for each pair; number squares for each pair

WHAT TO DO

● Each pair has a set of number cards. Shuffle and spread them face down on the table.

● Take it in turns to pick a card and say what number must be multiplied by 5 to make this total.

● If your partner agrees, you may keep the card. If not, return it to the table. If you disagree, use a number square to help decide whether an answer is correct.

● The winner is the player who has collected the most cards at the end of the game.

NOW TRY THIS

Use a mixed set of number cards (multiples of 2, 5 and 10). Think of a multiplication calculation in the two-, five- and ten-times tables which makes the number on the card that you have selected.

BAR OF CHOCOLATE

OBJECTIVE: to understand the operation of multiplication as representing an array
LEARNING LINK: visual
ORGANISATION: groups
RESOURCES: a large bar of chocolate, subdivided into smaller chunks; a plate; interlocking cubes pencils and paper for each group

WHAT TO DO

● Place a five-by-two block of chocolate on the plate. In your group, make the same bar of chocolate out of interlocking cubes.

● Write down the answers to the following questions:

How many rows of chocolate are there? (5)
How many pieces of chocolate are there in each row? (2)
How many pieces of chocolate are there altogether? (10)
If there were three rows, how many pieces of chocolate would there be? (15)

● One child in each group demonstrates how they counted in twos to work out the total number of chocolate pieces. Say together, *5 lots of 2 makes 10.*

● Your teacher will show you how to record the mental calculation as a number sentence ($5 \times 2 = 10$).

● Break the block of chocolate into two smaller pieces (three by two and two by two). Repeat the activity for each of these blocks of chocolate.

● Finally, if the chocolate bar is big enough, all the children can have a piece.

NOW TRY THIS

Prepare different arrays of interlocking cubes, such as seven by two, nine by two and one by two. Describe one of the arrays. Challenge the children to identify which block of cubes the description fits.

HOUSE OF STRAW

OBJECTIVE: to improve ability to count in fives; to solve simple mathematical problems
LEARNING LINK: visual
ORGANISATION: individuals or pairs
RESOURCES: art straws, cut into 5cm pieces

WHAT TO DO

● Use five straws to make a house.

● Make another house. Write down how many straws you have used altogether.

● Carry on building houses until you have a street of ten houses. How many straws have you used altogether? Did you remember to count the straws in fives?

NOW TRY THIS

1. Predict how many straws are needed to make 15 houses. Now build the houses to check your answer.

2. Use two straws to make a cross.

Investigate how many straws are needed to make, for example, 7 crosses or 12 crosses.

GEO BOARDS

OBJECTIVE: to improve ability to count in fives; to understand multiplication as repeated addition
LEARNING LINK: visual
ORGANISATION: individuals/pairs
RESOURCES: Geo boards and elastic bands

WHAT TO DO

● Work with a partner. Make a shape that has five corners.
● Now make a different shape with five corners. How many corners do the two shapes have altogether?
● Make as many different five-cornered shapes as you can. Count how many corners the shapes have altogether. Remember to count the corners in groups of five.
● Use a number line or hundred square to help you if you need it.

NOW TRY THIS

1. Draw five pentagons on a piece of dotty paper. How many sides do the shapes have altogether?
2. How many sides are there on eight pentagons, ten pentagons, and so on?

COUNTING HAT

OBJECTIVE: to improve ability to count in tens; to understand the operation of multiplication as repeated addition
LEARNING LINK: auditory
ORGANISATION: whole class
RESOURCES: a hat; sticky labels with multiples of 10 written on them

WHAT TO DO

● One child puts on the counting hat. Stick the number 60 on the hat.
● The child wearing the hat counts in tens until they reach 60.
● The rest of the class holds up a finger to represent each ten counted. Say together, *6 lots of 10 makes 60.*

● Repeat the activity. Different children wear the counting hat. Remember to stick a different number on the hat each time.

NOW TRY THIS

1. Count in fives until you reach the number on the counting hat.
2. Count in twos until you reach the number on the counting hat.
3. Work out how many twos you counted to reach 20. Write this as a number sentence.

TAP MY HAND

OBJECTIVE: to begin to derive and recall multiplication facts for the two-, five- and ten-times tables
LEARNING LINK: visual
ORGANISATION: pairs
RESOURCES: a number line; whiteboards and pens; a multiplication calculation written on the board, for example 4 × 5

WHAT TO DO

● In pairs, look at the calculation on the board. What does each number/symbol in the number sentence stand for?
● Work out the answer to the calculation with your partner. Tap your partner's hand four times. Ask your partner to count on five each time they feel a tap.
● Show your answer on a whiteboard.
● Swap roles. Look at the new calculation on the board. How many times do you need to tap your partner's hand to help them calculate the answer?

NOW TRY THIS

1. Tap your partner on the shoulder (or head) the correct number of times to help them work out the answer to the calculations on the board.
2. Work out the answer to some multiplication sums by making the right number of jumps on a number line.

KINAESTHETIC LEARNING

MONSTER FOOTPRINTS

OBJECTIVE: to improve ability to count in twos
LEARNING LINK: auditory
ORGANISATION: whole class, standing in a large space
RESOURCES: a small drum

WHAT TO DO

● Imagine that you are a monster in a muddy swamp.
● Move with heavy, two-footed jumps each time you hear the drum.
● After each beat of the drum, work out how many squelchy footprints you have made in the swamp.
● Are you counting in twos?

NOW TRY THIS

1. Try making footprints in the sand and snow.
2. How many jumps did it take the monster to make: 18 footprints?
   10 footprints?
   12 footprints?
   6 footprints?

COUNTING ACTIONS

OBJECTIVE: to improve ability to count in twos
LEARNING LINK: auditory
ORGANISATION: whole class, standing in a circle
RESOURCES: none required

WHAT TO DO

● Watch your teacher make a series of actions, for example clap, stamp, stamp, nod, nod. Join in when you can. Repeat the actions continuously until everybody is maintaining a steady rhythm.

● Count in twos from 2 in time with the actions, as follows. Continue counting in twos as far as you can.
● Repeat the activity with a new set of actions to accompany the counting.

NOW TRY THIS

1. Different children have a turn at being the leader and teach their own sequence of actions to the group.
2. Take it in turns around the circle to say the next number in the sequence and perform the action sequence.

PARK THE CAR

OBJECTIVE: to derive and recall multiplication facts for the two-times table
LEARNING LINK: auditory
ORGANISATION: whole class, in the playground or hall
RESOURCES: large number cards showing even numbers up to 20 (spread randomly face up on the floor)

WHAT TO DO

● Imagine that the playground is a giant car park and that each number represents a parking space.
● Pretend that you are driving around the car park looking for a space to park in. Unfortunately, all the spaces are full.
● Your teacher is the attendant in charge of the car park. The attendant will let you know when a space becomes free by calling out a calculation, for example 7 × 2. Work out the answer and drive to the correct space as quickly as you can.

NOW TRY THIS

1. Play the game again for the five- and ten-times tables.
2. Turn the activity into a knock-out game. The last person to drive to the correct car park space each time is out.
Continue until only one driver remains.

PASS THE PARCEL

OBJECTIVE: to practise counting on in twos from 0 to 20
LEARNING LINK: auditory
ORGANISATION: whole class, sitting in a circle
RESOURCES: a small prize that has been wrapped up in many layers; a number line

WHAT TO DO

● Practise counting in twos to 20 or beyond on the number line.
● Now you are going to play pass the parcel. The person who passes the parcel first says, 2. Each time the parcel is passed on, the person who passes it says the number that is two more (4), and so on.
● Continue passing the parcel around the circle and counting in twos in this way until the number 20 is reached. Whoever is holding the parcel at this point removes the outer layer of wrapping.
● Continue passing the parcel and counting in twos until someone unwraps the prize.

NOW TRY THIS

1. Predict who will say the number 20 each time.
2. Put a forfeit in each layer, for example, count in twos to 14.
3. Change the target number so that you can practise counting in twos beyond 20.

STATIONS

OBJECTIVE: to derive and recall multiplication facts for the ten-times table
LEARNING LINK: auditory
ORGANISATION: whole class, standing in a space in the hall or playground
RESOURCES: a whistle; four large number cards each showing a different multiple of ten, for example, 50, 90, 20, 30 (one in each corner of the room)

WHAT TO DO

● Pretend that you are a train moving along a track. The numbers in the corner of the room represent four different stations.

● When the whistle is blown, you start your engine and move around the room. When the whistle is blown again, you must move straight to a station and stand quietly.
● Your teacher will call out a calculation that corresponds to one of the number cards, for example 2 × 10. All the children standing at station 20 are out. Continue playing the game until only one train remains.

NOW TRY THIS

1. Adapt the game to practise recall of multiplication facts for the two- and five-times tables.
2. Play a variation of the stations game: pretend to be space rockets flying in space.

JUMP IN

OBJECTIVE: to derive and recall multiplication facts for the ten-times table
LEARNING LINK: auditory
ORGANISATION: whole class, sitting in a circle
RESOURCES: several sets of number cards, showing multiples of 10 to 100

WHAT TO DO

● Every child is dealt a card.
● Your teacher will call out a calculation from the ten-times table, for example 10 × 10. Jump in to the middle of the circle if you are holding the answer (100) and sit down.
● Different calculations are called out until everyone has jumped in and is sitting down.
● Swap number cards and play the game again. Jump into the circle in an imaginative way.

NOW TRY THIS

1. Each child holds a card with a calculation, for example 5 × 10. Jump in to the circle when the answer to your calculation is called out.
2. Throw a beanbag or ball into the circle if you are holding the answer to the questions.

EXPLODING TENS

OBJECTIVE: to improve ability to count in tens; to understand the operation of multiplication as repeated addition
LEARNING LINK: visual
ORGANISATION: whole class
RESOURCES: none required

WHAT TO DO

● Hold your hands out in front of you as fists. Practise 'exploding' ten fingers.
● Count to 100 in multiples of 10 as a class. Explode ten fingers to represent each 10 counted.
● Four children stand at the front of the class. Each child in turn silently explodes ten fingers while the rest of the class count in tens. How many lots of 10 make 40? Notice that the answer to the question is the number of children who exploded their fingers.
● Repeat for other multiples of 10.

NOW TRY THIS

1. Predict how many 'exploding tens' make, for example, 70. Check the answer by counting in tens while seven children explode ten fingers at the front of the class.
2. Count in twos. Punch both fists into the air to represent each two counted.
3. Count on in fives. Explode the fingers on each hand in turn.

HOT POTATO

OBJECTIVE: to derive and recall multiplication facts for the two-times table
LEARNING LINK: auditory
ORGANISATION: whole class, standing in a circle
RESOURCES: a beanbag

WHAT TO DO

● The beanbag is a hot potato. If anyone holds the hot potato for more than a few seconds, it will burn their fingers.
● Your teacher throws the hot potato to someone from the centre of the circle, calling out 5 x 2. If you catch the hot potato, throw it back, calling out the answer to the question at the same time.

● The hot potato is thrown to different children. A different multiplication is called out each time. Answer as quickly as possible so that the hot potato does not burn your fingers.

NOW TRY THIS

1. Turn the activity into a competitive game. If you answer incorrectly or take a long time to throw the beanbag back, you must sit down. The last few children standing are the winners.
2. Use different types of equipment to represent the hot potato such as a ball.

DICE CHALLENGE

OBJECTIVE: to begin to derive and recall multiplication facts for the two-, five- and ten-times tables
LEARNING LINK: visual
ORGANISATION: whole class or small groups
RESOURCES: a 1–6 dice (or 1–9, if available); a dice labelled 2, 2, 5, 5, 10, 10; a shuffled set of 0–100 number cards

WHAT TO DO

● Take it in turns as a class to roll both of the dice and multiply the two numbers together, for example 5 × 2.
● Record each child's score in a table on the board.
● Finally, pick a number card. The player who has made the number closest to the picked number is the winner. Look closely at the scores in the table to work out who the winner is.

NOW TRY THIS

1. Play the game with a partner. Record your scores in a table.
2. What numbers would you need to roll on the dice to score a total of 35 points? 12 points?
3. How many different ways could you score 20 using these dice?

SKITTLES

OBJECTIVE: to derive and recall multiplication facts for the two-times table; to improve ability to count in twos
LEARNING LINK: tactile
ORGANISATION: whole class or small groups
RESOURCES: ten skittles; three small balls; a small cone

WHAT TO DO

- The skittles are set up at one end of the room. The cone is placed a short distance away from the skittles to act as a marker to stand behind when it is your turn to play the game.
- Knock down as many skittles as you can by rolling the balls at the skittles one at a time. You will be awarded two points for each skittle you knock down.
- Calculate your score: How many skittles have you knocked down? (For example, 7.) What is 7 lots of 2? (14) If you are unable to recall the number fact from memory, work out your score by counting on in twos as each skittle you have knocked down is touched.
- Different children play skittles. Record everyone's score in a table on the board.

NOW TRY THIS
Solve these problems:
1. How many skittles would you need to knock down to score 8 points?
2. Sam knocked over 8 skittles. He scored 40 points. How many points did he score for each skittle he knocked over?

HOWZAT!

OBJECTIVE: to begin to know by heart multiplication facts for the two-, five- and ten-times tables
LEARNING LINK: auditory
ORGANISATION: whole class
RESOURCES: a cricket bat

WHAT TO DO

- You are going to play an imaginary game of cricket. One child is the batter. Take care to hold the cricket bat correctly!
- Four or five children are fielders. Practise jumping up to catch an imaginary ball.

- Your teacher is the bowler and bowls a question to the batter. The batter tries to 'hit' (shout) the answer back before the fielders 'catch' (shout) the correct answer.
- For example, 4 × 5 is bowled to the batter. If the batter shouts the correct answer first, they score a run and can stay in and have another go. If the fielders are first, the batter is out and must sit down. Another child takes over as the batter.
- At the end of each over (six balls), change fielders so that other children can have a go.

NOW TRY THIS
Play the game in small groups; use a set of question cards for the bowler to call out.

NUMBER RACE

OBJECTIVE: to derive and recall facts for the ten-times table
LEARNING LINK: auditory, visual
ORGANISATION: two or more teams in the playground or hall
RESOURCES: a set of A4-sized number cards showing multiples of 10 to 100 for each team

WHAT TO DO

- Sit in your teams at one end of the playground or hall.
- The number cards are spread out face up at the opposite end.
- Each team selects someone to take part in the first race. When a calculation from the ten-times table is called out, for example 7 × 10, the chosen children run to the opposite end and pick up the correct answer as quickly as they can. The first player to get back to their team, with the correct answer, scores a point for their team.
- The team with the most points at the end of the game is the winner.

NOW TRY THIS
1. Make the game more competitive by using just one set of number cards.
2. Adapt the game to practise facts for the two- and five-times tables.

HANDS IN

OBJECTIVE: to improve ability to count in fives; to begin to understand multiplication as repeated addition
LEARNING LINK: visual, auditory
ORGANISATION: whole class, sitting in a circle
RESOURCES: none required

WHAT TO DO

● Everyone sits in a circle with their hands behind their back.
● One child puts one hand into the circle, fingers outstretched. How many fingers are in the circle? The next child puts one hand into the circle and answers the question: How many fingers in the circle now? Do we need to count each finger? Practise counting in steps of five.
● Continue counting around the circle until everyone is holding one hand in the circle. Repeat the activity several times. Try to be ready for your turn and put your hand in and call out your number as quickly as you can.
● You might find it helpful to highlight the pattern of fives on a number line or hundred square.
● How many hands (lots of 5) do you need to put into the circle to make 15? 25? 40? 60?

NOW TRY THIS

1. Play 'Feet in' instead.
2. Play 'Hands and feet in'! Count in fives to larger numbers by putting both hands and feet into the circle.

MARCHING

OBJECTIVE: to improve ability to count in twos
LEARNING LINK: auditory
ORGANISATION: whole class
RESOURCES: a number line; a small drum

WHAT TO DO

● Count in twos from 0 to 20 or beyond. Point to the numbers on the number line – notice how you count every other number.
● Stand up and pretend that you are a soldier. Practise marching in time and standing to attention while your teacher beats a steady rhythm on the drum to 'The Grand Old Duke of York'.
● Starting from 0, count in twos together, in time with the marching beat. When you reach 20, look out for the signal to stop and stand to attention. Repeat several times.

● Individual soldiers stand at the front where they march and count in twos in time with the drum until the signal for them to stop and stand to attention is given.

NOW TRY THIS

1. March to the beat while counting in fives or tens.
2. Accompany the count with other body actions, for example jumps or turns.

FINGERS AND TOES

OBJECTIVE: to improve ability to count in tens
LEARNING LINK: visual, tactile
ORGANISATION: all children, standing in a space in the hall
RESOURCES: a CD player and a lively piece of music

WHAT TO DO

● Dance to the music that is playing. Whenever the music stops, stop dancing and stand still. When you hear a number called out, for example 3, you must get into groups of this size as quickly as you can. Practise this several times.
● Play the game again, but this time when the music stops and you have got into groups, work out how many fingers and toes are in your group altogether. The first group to shout out the correct answer is the winner.
● A member of the winning group has to explain how they calculated the answer each time. Notice that it is much quicker to calculate the answer by counting in tens, than by counting in ones.

NOW TRY THIS

1. How many arms and eyes are there in your group?
2. Get into a group with 50 toes or 10 eyes.

FIREWORKS

OBJECTIVE: to recognise two digit multiples of ten
LEARNING LINK: auditory
ORGANISATION: whole class
RESOURCES: none required

WHAT TO DO

● Crouch down on the floor. Count together in hushed voices, 1, 2, 3... until number 10 is reached. Shout 10! as loudly as you can while simultaneously jumping up and pretending to explode like a firework.
● Drop back to a crouched position and continue counting quietly, 11, 12, 13... all the way to 100. Jump up and explode like a firework on every multiple of ten.

NOW TRY THIS

1. 'Explode' on multiples of 5 or multiples of 2.
2. Play percussion instruments as loudly as you can on every multiple of ten.

FIND YOUR PARTNER

OBJECTIVE: to begin to derive and recall multiplication facts for the two- and ten-times tables
LEARNING LINK: visual
ORGANISATION: whole class, split into two groups (A and B)
RESOURCES: 20 A5-sized cards with a different multiplication calculation of ten of the cards (for example 2 × 5, 6 × 10) and the corresponding answers on the remaining ten cards (use different-coloured card for the questions and answers)

WHAT TO DO

● Children in Group A stand in a space. Each has an answer card to hold up.

● Each child in Group B has a question card; they have a minute to work out the answer to the multiplication calculation on their card. When your teacher shouts *Find your partner!*, the children in Group B go and stand by the child in Group A who is holding up the answer to their question – as fast as they can.
● If everyone has found their correct partner, swap cards and play again.

NOW TRY THIS

Use the cards to play multiplication snap in pairs.

IN THE RING

OBJECTIVE: to improve ability to count in fives; to begin to know multiplication facts for the five-times table
LEARNING LINK: tactile
ORGANISATION: small groups
RESOURCES: a large hoop for each group; a beanbag for each child; a score board

WHAT TO DO

● Everyone in your group stands around the hoop and throws their beanbag into it.
● Count how many beanbags land in the hoop altogether. Calculate the group's score by multiplying the number of beanbags in the hoop by five.
● Check that the score is correct by lifting the beanbags out of the hoop one at a time and counting in fives.
● Repeat several times. A different child checks the score each time.

NOW TRY THIS

1. Throw balls into a bucket. Award two points for each ball that lands in the bucket.
2. Kick footballs into a net. Award ten points for each goal scored.

WALK THE PLANK

OBJECTIVE: to derive and recall multiplication facts for the two- and ten-times tables
LEARNING LINK: auditory
ORGANISATION: whole class; small groups
RESOURCES: a simple pirate costume, for example an eye patch and a headscarf; a wooden PE bench; PE mats (PE mats are arranged into a rectangle large enough for all of the children to sit on, the bench is at a right angle to the mats)

WHAT TO DO

● You are prisoners on a pirate ship. Your teacher is a pirate. All the prisoners are going to walk the plank.
● Each prisoner stands on the bench in turn. They will be asked a times table question by the pirate, for example 7 x 2. If the question is answered correctly the prisoner can go free. If the wrong answer is given, they must walk the plank to the end!

NOW TRY THIS

Set a time limit. You must answer the question/s you are set within the set time.

DRIBBLING

OBJECTIVE: to improve ability to count in tens
LEARNING LINK: visual, auditory
ORGANISATION: whole class, working individually in the playground or hall
RESOURCES: small footballs; cones; large number cards showing multiples of 10 to 100

WHAT TO DO

● There is a number card on each cone. The cones are in order 0, 10, 20 and so on.
● This game is played one child at a time.
● Stand beside the cone marked 0. Dribble the football around each of the cones in turn. Shout out the number on each cone as you dribble the ball round it: 0, 10, 20, and so on.

● Try the task again when the cones are spread randomly in the available space. Make sure that you dribble around the cones in order, starting from 0.

NOW TRY THIS

Download or create your own multiples of 10 dot-to-dot puzzles. Join the dots in order to complete a picture or pattern.

FITNESS CIRCUIT

OBJECTIVE: to improve ability to count in steps of ones, twos, fives or tens
LEARNING LINK: auditory
ORGANISATION: four groups in the hall
RESOURCES: giant number cards (1, 2, 5, 10); a whistle; skipping ropes; hoops; big balls; beanbags

WHAT TO DO

● There is a number card and a set of equipment in each corner of the hall. The activities in the fitness circuit are:
1. Skipping with a skipping rope
2. Bouncing a big ball
3. Tossing a beanbag from one hand to the other
4. Jumping in and out of a hoop.
● You will work in four groups. Each group starts with a different activity in the fitness circuit.
● While performing each of the different activities, chant on in steps of one, two, five or ten, according to the number card displayed in each corner.
● When the whistle blows, after three or four minutes, move on to the next activity. Continue until you have completed the fitness circuit.

NOW TRY THIS

'Counting aerobics': a whole-class fitness session. Count in twos, fives or tens. Perform an exercise every time a number is chanted.

SEWING

OBJECTIVE: to improve ability to count on in twos from 0 to 20
LEARNING LINK: visual
ORGANISATION: whole class, then individual
RESOURCES: sewing cards numbered 0–20; needles and thread

WHAT TO DO
- Count in twos from 0 to 20.
- Start with a multiple of two, for example 6. Say the multiple of two that comes after 6. Repeat for other multiples of two up to 20.
- Each child has a sewing card, a needle and some thread.
- Using your sewing card, push your needle and thread up through the hole numbered 0 and then sew through the remaining holes in order up to 20.

NOW TRY THIS
1. Download or create your own multiples of two dot-to-dot puzzles. Join the dots in order to complete a picture or pattern.
2. Use a different sewing card on which the holes are numbered in multiples of 10 from 0 to 100.

THROW AND CATCH

OBJECTIVE: to improve ability to count in fives; to begin to understand the operation of multiplication as repeated addition
LEARNING LINK: auditory
ORGANISATION: whole class, working in pairs
RESOURCES: a beanbag, a score sheet, a pencil and a hundred square for each pair

WHAT TO DO
- Play 'Throw and catch' with a partner. Count in fives as the beanbag passes back and forth.
- If either of you drops the beanbag, stop and record your score in the first column on the score sheet.

- After about five minutes, group together with another pair. One pair tells the other their highest score, for example 45. Make jumps of five on the hundred square to work out how many times this pair caught the beanbag to make this total.
- Add the number of catches to the second column on the score sheet.
- Write up other pairs' scores.

NOW TRY THIS
1. Kick the ball to each other while counting in tens.
2. Hit a tennis ball back and forth while counting in twos.

CHANGING PLACES

OBJECTIVE: to begin to recognise multiples of two, five and ten; to begin derive and recall multiplication facts for the two- five- and ten times tables
LEARNING LINK: visual
ORGANISATION: whole class, sitting in a circle
RESOURCES: large number cards showing multiples of 2, 5 and 10 (enough for all the class to have one card)

WHAT TO DO
- Sit in a circle with one child standing in the centre
- Everyone is dealt a number card, except the child in the middle. Place your number card face up on the floor in front of you.
- The child in the middle has to follow the instruction that is called out, such as, *Change places with a number that is a multiple of five.*
- Continue the game following instructions of varying difficulty. For example, *Change places with a multiple of two that is greater than twenty. Change places with the number that is 4 times 5. Change places with the number that is missing from this sequence: 2, 4 _, 8.*

NOW TRY THIS
Try following instructions that require several members of the group to get up and change places at the same time. For example, *Multiples of 5, all change.*

CHANGING PLACES RACE

OBJECTIVE: to derive and recall multiplication facts for the two- and ten-times tables
LEARNING LINK: visual
ORGANISATION: whole class, standing in a circle with two children in the middle
RESOURCES: large number cards showing multiples of 2 and 10 (enough for every child to have a card)

WHAT TO DO

● Everyone in the circle has a number card. Place your number card face up on the floor in front of you.

● Your teacher will call out a multiplication calculation, for example, 7 x 2. The two children in the middle must race to find the answer. Whoever locates the number first should swap places with the child who is standing by that number.

● Repeat with different multiplication calculations until everyone has had at least one turn in the middle.

NOW TRY THIS

1. Play with three children in the middle, who all have to race to find the answer.
2. Use a range of vocabulary, for example, 7 lots of 2, 9 times 2, 7 multiplied by 10.

BALANCING

OBJECTIVE: to improve ability to count in fives to 20 and beyond; to begin to know multiplication facts for the five-times table
LEARNING LINK: tactile
ORGANISATION: whole class, standing in a large space
RESOURCES: a dice numbered 0, 5, 10, 15, 15, 20

WHAT TO DO

● Count your fingers and toes in fives. The word 'digit' is often used when talking about fingers and toes. How many digits are there on one hand? How many digits are there on one hand and two feet? Agree that there are 15 digits.

● One child rolls the dice and calls out the number. Make an interesting balance with that number of digits touching the floor.

● Look at the different combinations of hands and feet that other children have used.

● Another child rolls the dice. Repeat the activity.

NOW TRY THIS

Work in pairs. Balance with the appropriate number of digits on the floor when multiples of 5, from 10 to 40, are called out.

ROW YOUR BOAT

OBJECTIVE: to begin to recognise multiples of two, five and ten
LEARNING LINK: visual
ORGANISATION: whole class, in the hall
RESOURCES: giant number cards (2, 5,10); smaller number cards showing different multiples of 2, 5 and 10 (one card for each pair)

WHAT TO DO

● The large number cards are in different corners of the room.

● Sit down in a space with a partner. Pretend that you have hired a rowing boat on a lake. Sing 'Row, row your boat'. While you are singing, a number card will be placed beside you.

● At the end of the song your teacher will say, *Come in please – your time is up.* Everyone must return their boats to the correct mooring. Look at the number card beside your boat, decide whether you think the number is a multiple of two, five or ten, and then row your boat to the correct corner of the hall.

● Check to see whether you are all standing in the correct place. (Remember that some of the numbers are multiples of 2 and 10, 5 and 10 or even 2, 5 and 10.)

● Find a new partner and play the game again.

NOW TRY THIS

Sort a set of number cards into multiples of 2, 5 or 10 as quickly as you can.

STEPPING STONES

OBJECTIVE: to derive and recall multiplication facts for the ten-times table
LEARNING LINK: visual
ORGANISATION: whole class
RESOURCES: 11 cardboard stepping stones with a multiplication calculation (0×10 to 10×10) on one side of each stepping stone, and the corresponding answer on the reverse

WHAT TO DO

- The whole class sits at one side of the classroom or hall.
- Six stepping stones are in a line in front of the class (calculation side up). The stepping stones are the only safe way to cross to the other side of a crocodile-infested river.
- A brave volunteer attempts to cross the river. The volunteer stands on the river bank in front of the first stepping stone and reads and answers the calculation on the first stone. The answer can be checked by turning the stepping stone over.
- If they have answered the question correctly, they may proceed onto the stepping stone and continue. If they have got the answer wrong, they are eaten by crocodiles.
- See how many children can safely cross the stepping stones. Use a new set of stepping stones each time.

NOW TRY THIS

1. Practise quick recall of times table facts, crossing the river within a set time limit.
2. Use other sets of stepping stones to practise recall of facts for the two- and five-times tables.

LAST ONE STANDING

OBJECTIVE: to count on in fives from 0
LEARNING LINK: auditory
ORGANISATION: whole class
RESOURCES: a beanbag or small class toy

WHAT TO DO

- Highlight the pattern of fives to 50 on the number line. What do you notice about these numbers? All the numbers end with a 5 or a 0.

- Stand in a circle. Play 'Last one standing'. Pass the beanbag around the circle while, at the same time, counting in unison to 50 in steps of five. The child holding the beanbag when the number 50 is reached should sit down. They are now out of the game, but must keep counting with the the class.
- Continue counting in fives and passing the beanbag around the circle of children still standing.
- The child who is the 'Last one standing' is the winner.

NOW TRY THIS

1. Predict who will have to sit down at the end of each turn.
2. Practise counting in fives to larger totals. For example, the child who is holding the beanbag when 100 is reached should sit down.

TWOS RACE

OBJECTIVE: to improve ability to count in twos
LEARNING LINK: visual
ORGANISATION: whole class, divided into four teams, in the hall
RESOURCES: a set of number cards showing the even numbers from 2–20 for each team; four different-coloured hoops

WHAT TO DO

- The class is divided into four teams. Each group sits in a different corner of the hall. The hoops are in the centre of the room. There is a shuffled set of number cards in each hoop.
- When your teacher shouts *go!*, one member of each team must run to their hoop, pick up a number card and bring it back to their team.
- As soon as the first child comes back, the next child runs to fetch a card and so on.
- The winning team is the first to collect all the multiples of 2 and arrange them in the correct order.

NOW TRY THIS

1. Collect the multiples of 2 in the correct order.
2. Repeat the activity, using multiples of 5 and 10.

DRESSING-UP BOX

OBJECTIVE: to derive and recall addition doubles of all numbers up to ten

LEARNING LINK: auditory

ORGANISATION: whole class, sitting in a circle

RESOURCES: a small ball; a box of dressing-up clothes, for example hats, scarves, glasses

WHAT TO DO

● Your teacher rolls the ball to a child in the circle, and calls out a number between 1 and 10. The child with the ball calls out the number that is double the starting number as they return the ball.

● If the child doubles the number correctly, they can choose an item from the dressing-up box and put it on. Continue until all children are wearing an item from the dressing-up box.

NOW TRY THIS

Play the game just before playtime with everyone's coats in the middle of the circle. See how quickly everyone can be ready for playtime.

CHOCOLATE CHALLENGE

OBJECTIVE: to derive and recall addition doubles of all numbers to six

LEARNING LINK: visual

ORGANISATION: whole class, sitting in a circle

RESOURCES: a hat, scarf and gloves; a tray; a bar of chocolate; a knife and fork; two large 1–6 dice (spots or numerals)

WHAT TO DO

● All of the equipment is in the centre of the circle. One child rolls the dice first. If a double is rolled, they shout out the total number of spots as quickly as they can. They put on the hat, scarf and gloves and use the knife and fork to try and break off a piece of chocolate.

● At the same time, the rest of the class continues to pass the dice around the circle, taking it in turns to try to roll a double. As soon as someone rolls a double and correctly calls out the total number of spots, they may go into the middle of the circle and try and get some chocolate.

● Continue until all of the chocolate has been eaten.

NOW TRY THIS

Your teacher puts several sets of dominoes into a bag. Take it in turns to pull a domino out of the bag until someone gets a double.

JUMPING IN TWOS

OBJECTIVE: to practise recording mental calculations in a number sentence

LEARNING LINK: visual

ORGANISATION: individuals or pairs

RESOURCES: a hundred square large enough for the children to step on; paper and pencils

WHAT TO DO

● Start at 0. Step on every other number on the hundred square as you count in twos.

● Write down directions for a partner. Tell them how to get from 0 to number 8 by jumping in twos. ($2 + 2 + 2 + 2 = 8$ or $4 \times 2 = 8$)

● Check the directions are correct by jumping on the giant hundred square.

● Work with your partner. Choose different even numbers that you would like to land on. Write down instructions for getting those numbers by counting in twos.

NOW TRY THIS

Swap instructions with another pair of children. Follow the directions on the hundred square. Which number do you land on?

ADD IT UP

OBJECTIVE: to understand multiplication as repeated addition
LEARNING LINK: visual
ORGANISATION: groups of two to four
RESOURCES: a dice or spinner numbered 2, 2, 5, 5, 10, 10, and a set of instruction cards for each group; paper and pencils (the cards should read 'Add the number on the dice 2 times.', 'Add the number on the dice 3 times.', and so on, up to 'Add the number on the dice 6 times.')

WHAT TO DO

● Each group shuffles their cards and spreads them face down on the table.
● Take it in turns to turn over a card, roll the dice and record the calculation. For example, 10 + 10 + 10 + 10 = 40.
● Once everyone in your group has had a turn, compare calculations. The child with the highest total scores a point. Return the cards to the table, ready for the next round.
● The winner is the child with the most points at the end of the game.

NOW TRY THIS

1. In addition to recording an addition number sentence, use the symbols × and = to record the corresponding multiplication calculation.
2. Play the game using instruction cards up to 'Add the number on the dice 10 times.'

CHASE AROUND THE CIRCLE

OBJECTIVE: To improve ability to count on in steps of 2, 5 and 10
LEARNING LINK: auditory
ORGANISATION: whole class
RESOURCES: none required

WHAT TO DO

● Everyone sits in a circle in the hall or playground. You are going to play a chasing game. If you are chosen to play this is what you must do.

● Your teacher will call out a number, for example '25, 15, 30'. Stand up and walk around the circle in a clockwise direction. Gently pat each child that you pass on the head. Starting from 5, count on 5 more as you pat each child on the head. The child who you pat as you say 25 stands up and chases you around the circle. Run as fast as you can. Can you get back to your place without getting caught?

NOW TRY THIS

1. The target number is changed to a multiple of 2 or 10 so that you can practise counting in two or tens.
1. Play this variation of the game:
Several sets of number cards, showing even numbers from 2–20, are shuffled together. Everyone in the circle is dealt a number card. Place your number card on the floor in front of you.
Your teacher will call out a multiplication calculation for example, '7x2'. Any children with the number 14 must stand up and race around the circle. Whoever is first back to their place is the winner.

ISLANDS

OBJECTIVE: to know by heart doubles of all numbers to at least 10.
LEARNING LINK: auditory
ORGANISATION: whole class
RESOURCES: 10 hoops spread out in the hall or playground, large number cards showing even numbers to 20

WHAT TO DO

● Stand inside a hoop. The hoops are islands in a shark-infested sea. Each island has a number. Unfortunately the islands are made from quicksand and every so often one of the islands disappears into the sea. Anyone who is on that island is eaten by sharks.
● Swim around the islands. When you hear your teacher shout 'SHARKS ARE COMING!' swim to the nearest island. Your teacher will call out a question e.g. double 8. Anyone standing on island number 16 is out.
● Carry on playing the game until only one child remains.

NOW TRY THIS

1. Play a variation of the game to practise times table facts for the 2, 5 or 10.

Name _____ Date _____

Multiple football gameboard

Multiples of 2

Multiples of 5

Multiples of 10

DAILY TIMES TABLES TEASERS **FOR AGES 5–7**

Name _____ Date _____

Treasure Island

- Work out the answer to the clues below.
- Locate the squares on the grid with the answers to the clues on them. Mark the squares with a coloured cross.
- Record the pathway to the treasure by drawing a line from one answer to the next.

Clues:

7 x 2 = ☐

0 x 2 = ☐

3 x 10 = ☐

2 x 8 = ☐

0 x 10 = ☐

2 x 2 = ☐

6 x 10 = ☐

10 x 10 = ☐

2 x 6 = ☐

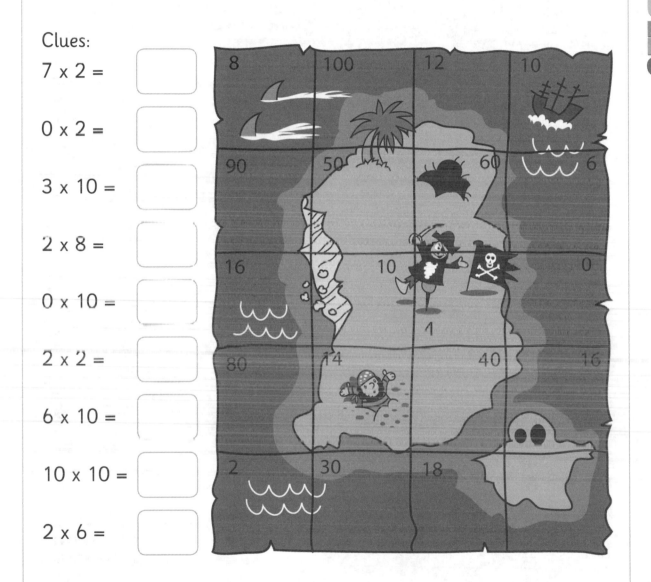

57

PHOTOCOPIABLES

PHOTOCOPIABLE

Growing wild

A plant is 2cm tall on Monday. It grows 2cm each day. Write and draw how tall the plant is on each day of the week. How tall is the plant on Saturday?

Monday: 2cm	Tuesday:	Wednesday:	Thursday:	Friday:	Saturday:

Name _____ Date _____

Name _____ Date _____

Crack the code

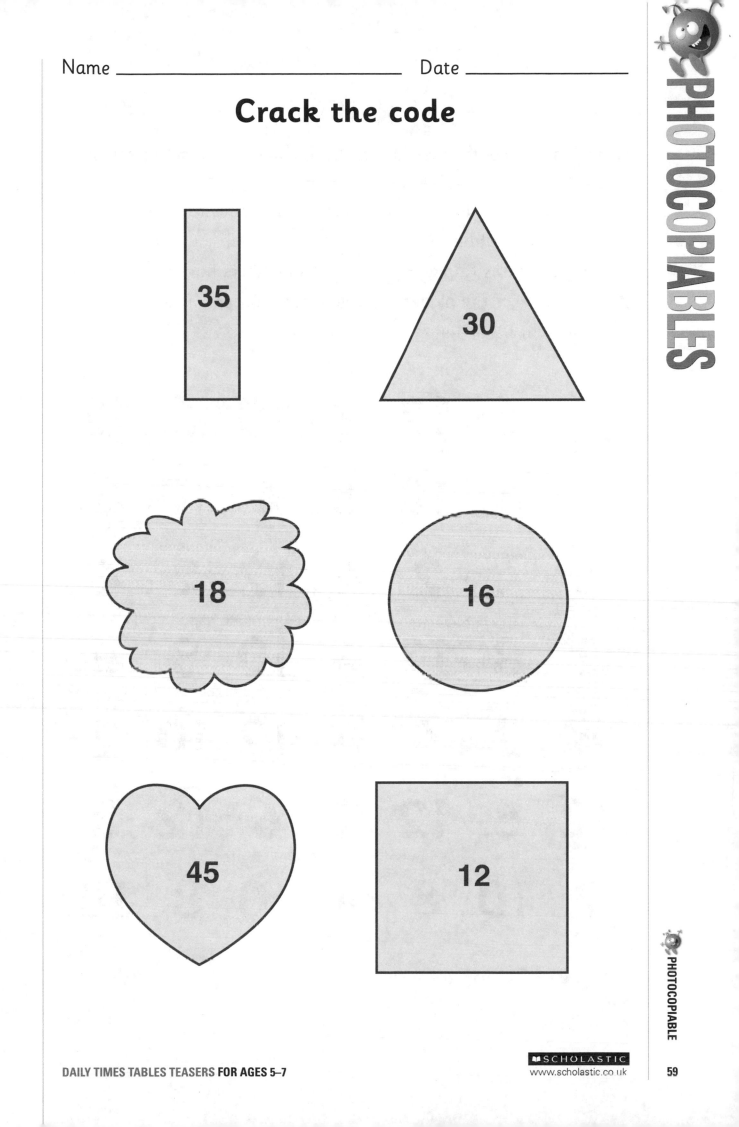

Name _____   Date _____

Roll it!

- This is a game for two players. Each player has a set of coloured counters.
- Roll the dice and multiply the number you have rolled by two.
- Cover the total on the board with one of your counters.
- Take it in turns to play until all of the numbers have been covered.
- The winner is the player with the most counters on the board at the end of the game.

2	6	12	2	10	6	12
4	8	10	6	4	10	8
6	4	2	4	12	2	4
2	8	12	6	10	8	6
4	2	4	8	12	10	2
12	6	12	2	6	12	8
2	10	8	4	10	8	10

Name _____ Date _____

Make a face

- The aim of the game is to be the first person to draw a face with two eyes, two ears, a nose, a mouth and some hair.

- Take it in turns to roll the dice, double the number of spots shown and then look on the game card to see which facial feature you can draw.

- You must score 12 and draw a face before you can begin to collect the other facial features.

SCHOLASTIC
www.scholastic.co.uk

PHOTOCOPIABLES

PHOTOCOPIABLE

Name _____ Date _____

Beans

Use the beans on your table to investigate which numbers can be grouped into piles of five and ten. Complete the table below.

Number of beans	Can be grouped in fives (✓)	Can be grouped in tens (✓)
15		
5		
13		
10		
30		
7		
20		

SCHOLASTIC www.scholastic.co.uk

DAILY TIMES TABLES TEASERS **FOR AGES 5–7**

Name _____ Date _____

Add it up

Copy one set of instruction cards per group onto thin card.

Add the number on the dice 2 times.

Add the number on the dice 3 times.

Add the number on the dice 4 times.

Add the number on the dice 5 times.

Add the number on the dice 6 times.

■SCHOLASTIC
www.scholastic.co.uk

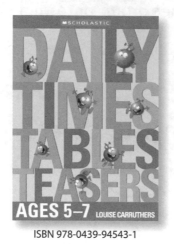

■SCHOLASTIC

Also available in this series:

ISBN 978-0439-94543-1

ISBN 978-0439-94544-8

ISBN 978-0439-96542-2

ISBN 978-0439-96543-9

ISBN 978-0439-96544-6

To find out more, call: 0845 603 9091
or visit our website www.scholastic.co.uk